VOL.2

SCRAPS, INC.

I5 SCRAP-PIECED DESIGNS FOR THE MODERN QUILTER

Compiled by
Susanne Woods

Published in 2015 by Lucky Spool Media, LLC

Lucky Spool Media, LLC
1005 Blackwood Lane, Lafayette, CA 94549
www.luckyspool.com
info@luckyspool.com

TEXT © Individual Designers
EDITOR Susanne Woods
ILLUSTRATIONS Kari Vojtechovsky
PHOTOGRAPHY © Nydia Kenhle
DESIGNER Kari Vojtechovsky
FRONT COVER DESIGN BASED ON DESIGN BY Liz Quan

The information in this book is accurate and complete to the best
of our knowledge. All recommendations are made without guarantee
on the part of the author of Lucky Spool Media, LLC. The author and
publisher disclaim any liability in connection with this information.

Note to copy shops: Pages 118–127 can be photocopied for personal use.

Photograph on cover and page 8 © Kari Vojtechovsky
Photograph on page 15 of Alex Ledgerwood © Lauren Hunt
Photograph on page 41 of April Rosenthal © VIS-A-VIS Studio
Photograph on page 47 of Dorie Schwarz © Eva Schwarz
Photograph on page 79 of Kari Vojtechovsky © Andrew Kowalyshyn
Photograph on page 95 of Katie Blakesley © Mary Clark of DMC Studios
Photograph on page 101 of Melissa Lunden © Peter Ellenby
Photograph on page 107 of Nydia Kenhle © Teddy Rodriguez Photography
Photograph on page 113 of Sherri McConnell © Korindi Totten

9 8 7 6 5 4 3 2 1

First Edition
Printed and bound in China

Library of Congress Cataloging-in-Publication Data available upon request

ISBN: 978-1-940655-19-2
LSID 0025

CONTENTS

Welcome   7

Basic Blocks   8

PROJECTS

1: Twirligig   14

By Alex Ledgerwood

2: Letterpress   22

By Allison Harris

3: Fletching   28

By Amy Friend

4: Scrap Bag Stars   34

By Amy Smart

5: Square-Rific!   40

By April Rosenthal

6: Chimney Swifts   46

By Dorie Schwarz

7: Argyle Medallion   54

By Erin Burke Harris

8: Sweet Emmeline   64

By Janice Zeller Ryan

9: Origami Garden   72

By John Adams

10: You+Me+Us   78

By Kari Vojtechovsky

11: Confetti   86

By Kati Spencer

12: Division Street Diamonds   94

By Katie Blakesley

13: Northern Migration   100

By Melissa Lunden

14: Blacklight   106

By Nydia Kehnle

15: California Dreamin'   112

By Sherri McConnell

Templates   118

Welcome to

SCRAPS, INC.

If you picked up this book, you are probably already a prolific quilt maker, with a love for each and every inch of the leftover fabrics from each and every quilt you've made. This has likely turned you into one of us: a scrap junkie.

We know who we are. We are the ones who happily create a myriad of storage solutions for all our scraps. We are the ones who look secretly and fondly through our scrap bins way more often than we should. We are the ones who buy, swap, and trade scraps among our fellow obsessives. So, if you are one of us, this is the book for you.

Scraps, Inc. Vol. 2 features 15 of the best designers in quilt-making today and the scrappy patterns they created just for this book. We know that scrappy quilts are often the ones you keep for yourself, so we wanted to offer a series of designs that would fit well in any home.

In each of the chapters, the designer also introduces you to his or her own favorite past Inspired Scraps project that they enjoyed making. We hope you check out the websites, tutorials and books that our designers love and that their stories continue to keep you inspired. Most of all, we hope that you rummage through your scrap bins and rediscover why you treasured each piece of fabric as you sew one or many of these stunning project quilts.

BASIC BLOCKS

Here are some basic techniques that you will find helpful in the projects. Since this book is about scraps, it is our assumption that you have already learned the basics of quilt making and have discovered certain techniques and methods of construction that have become your favorites. However, if this is your first quilt-making book or even if you just need a reminder on some of the basics, please check out the free PDF available at luckyspool.com containing our Quilt Making Basics.

HALF-SQUARE TRIANGLE (AKA HST)

Gather a Fabric A square and a Fabric B square. This example creates 2½'' pieces. Refer to your pattern instructions for the precise unit measurements.

Figure 1.   *Figure 2.*   *Figure 3.*

1 Cut (2) 3'' squares of Fabric A and (2) 3'' squares of Fabric B.

2 Using a water-soluble marker and an acrylic ruler, draw a diagonal line on the wrong side of each Fabric A square. (Fig. 1)

3 Pair each marked Fabric A square with a Fabric B square, right sides together. On each pair, sew ¼'' away from both sides of the marked diagonal.

4 Cut along the drawn diagonal line, fold open along the seam line, and you have half-square triangle units. (Fig. 2)

5 Set the seams with a hot iron and press toward the darker fabric. Trim as needed. (Fig. 3)

FLYING GEESE

Gather one rectangle of Fabric A and two smaller squares of Fabric B. Refer to your pattern instructions for the precise unit measurements.

Figure 4.   *Figure 5.*

1 Using a water-soluble marker and an acrylic ruler, draw a diagonal line on the wrong side of both small Fabric B squares.

2 With right sides together, position a marked square on the left side of a Fabric A rectangle. The drawn line should go from the top left corner to the bottom right corner of the square. (Fig. 4)

3 Sew on the diagonal line.

4 Trim to the left of the sewn line, leaving a ¼'' seam allowance. Press the triangle open.

5 Repeat for opposite side of the rectangle with the second square. This time, the diagonal line should go from the bottom left to the top right of the square. Trim to the right of the sew line (Fig. 5). Press.

PAPER PIECING

1 To practice, make a 6½'' square on a piece of copy paper. Center a 6'' square inside. From the lower left corner of the inner square, draw 4 lines using Figure 6 as a reference and number each section. Cut your fabric a little bigger than you normally would for machine piecing. Beginning with Section 1, pin your fabric to the wrong side of the template, making sure that you have at least ¼'' of fabric extending past the drawn lines. (Fig. 7)

2 After ensuring that your fabric selection for Section 2 also has at least ¼'' around all sides (hold the layers up to a sunny window to check), place the fabric for Section 2 on top of the fabric for Section 1, right sides together. Pin in place if needed. Flip over your template so that the numbers are facing you and the fabric is on the bottom.

3 Set your machine's stitch length to 1.5mm. This will make removal of the template paper a lot easier. Sew along the line between Sections 1 and 2, extending into the seam allowance.

4 Fold the paper along the sewn line so that the right sides of the paper are facing. Use a ruler to measure ¼'' away from the sewn line onto the exposed fabric. Trim excess fabric with a rotary cutter and press open.

5 Repeat for all sections of the template, working in numerical order. (Fig. 8)

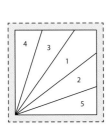

Figure 6.

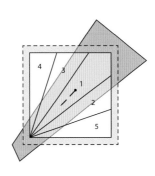

Figure 7.

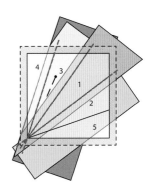

Figure 8.

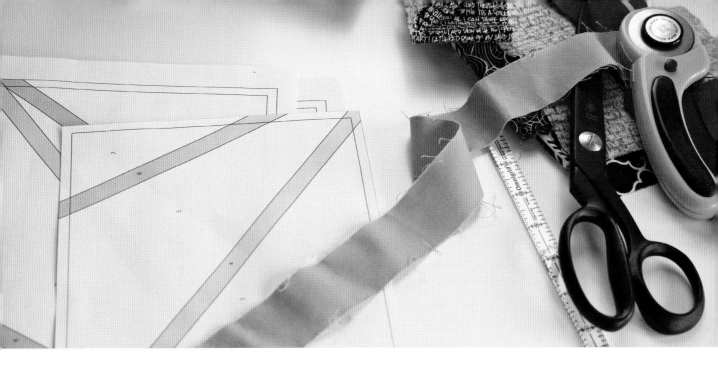

6 Press all seams again, this time on the right side of the fabric. (Fig. 9)

7 With the paper side facing up, trim around the template. Make sure to include any marked seam allowances. (Fig. 10)

You did it! If you are working on a larger project with many paper-pieced components, you may want to wait until the top is completely assembled before removing the paper. If not, carefully remove the paper from the back, being careful not to distort the shape.

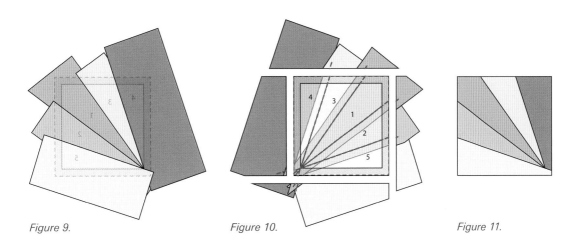

Figure 9.

Figure 10.

Figure 11.

THE PROJECTS

Made with
SQUARES

TWIRLIGIG

Simple, improv arcs, cut by hand and appliquéd onto strips of background fabric become twirling strands of color. The movement in this bold, modern quilt comes from the simple design choice of offsetting the arc shapes, creating the illusion of spinning, cascading curves. Use needle turn appliqué or your favorite appliqué method to attach the arcs. Cut from your scraps and combine with a soft linen background farbic to create this simple but dynamic design.

By Alex Ledgerwood

Finished Quilt Size: 56"×72"

MATERIALS

Scraps: Assorted scraps in purple, pink, orange, and gray for a total of 40–48 rectangles ranging from 3''×4'' to 6½''×8''

Background Fabric: 3½ yards

Binding Fabric: ½ yard

Backing Fabric: 4½ yards

Batting: 64''×80''

CUTTING

Note: Width of Fabric = WOF

From Scraps, cut:
- rectangles or squares between 3'' and 8'' but no taller than 6¼'' on one edge

From the Background Solid, cut:
- (4) 4½''×WOF strips
- (8) 6½''×40½'' strips
- (7) 6½''×WOF strips; subcut into:
  - (1) 30½''×6½'' rectangle
  - (1) 26½''×6½'' rectangle
  - (1) 24½''×6½'' rectangle
  - (1) 20½''×6½'' rectangle
  - (1) 19½''×6½'' rectangle
  - (1) 17½''×6½'' rectangle
  - (2) 16½''×6½'' rectangles
  - (1) 15½''×6½'' rectangle
  - (1) 13½''×6½'' rectangle
  - (1) 12½''×6½'' rectangle
  - (1) 8½''×6½'' rectangle
  - (1) 7½''×6½'' rectangle
  - (1) 6½'' square
  - (1) 2½''×6½'' rectangle
  - (1) 25½''×6½'' rectangle

From the Binding Fabric, cut:
- (7) 2½''×WOF strips

QUILTER TO QUILTER

The two border strips on each side of the quilt are 4½''×72½'' unfinished. I recommend that you join two WOF strips and then trim them to the required length. If you prefer a strip that is not pieced, adjust the yardage requirements accordingly, but if cut on the length of the fabric instead of the width, the grain-line will be different. Because of this, the latter method is not appropriate for linen or directional background fabrics.

CREATING THE APPLIQUÉ STRIPS

To make each appliqué strip you will need:
- *1 strip of background fabric 6½"×40½"*
- *5 or more scrap rectangles or squares*

1 Fold each scrap in half, with the folded edge measuring no more than 6¼". Using scissors, cut a gently curved half arc, freehand. Vary the shapes on the arcs for interest by making the arcs narrow, tall, wide or short. (Fig. 1)

2 Unfold the arcs and arrange as desired along one long edge of the background strip. Pin the arcs in place.

3 Baste the arcs to the background, right sides up and keeping the basting stitches ¼" from the arcs' edges. (Fig. 2)

4 Using a coordinating thread, appliqué the arcs to the background leaving the straight edge unsewn (it will be sewn into the seam in a later step). Sweep the curved raw edge under about ⅛" with your needle, until it meets the basting stitches, just a half inch ahead of your last stitch, making small stitches every ⅛" or so. (Fig. 3)

5 Remove the basting stitches along the curved edges. (Fig. 4)

6 Repeat to create all eight appliqué strips.

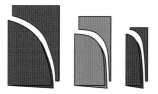

Figure 1.

Figure 2.

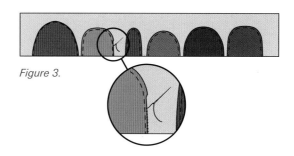

Figure 3.

Figure 4.

QUILTER TO QUILTER

Use your favorite appliqué method to sew the arcs onto the background fabric. But, if you haven't tried needle turn appliqué before, I encourage you to on this project. Because the arcs are gentle curves cut free hand, making each one different, they are a very forgiving shape for those new to the technique.

SEWING THE COLUMNS

1 Referencing Figure 5, arrange columns 1–8. Position the appliqué strips as desired.

2 Once you have finalized your strip placement, sew the columns together following the chart below and working from top to bottom.

QUILTER TO QUILTER

A design wall is very helpful at this stage of the quilt construction, but the floor works too. Play with the order of your strips to achieve a nice distribution of color and value. I recommend placing your background strips first, then auditioning the arc strips in different positions.

Column Piecing Order

Column	1	2	3	4	5	6	7	8
Top Background Rectangle	2½''×6½''	8½''×6½''	26½''×6½''	16½''×6½''	7½''×6½''	17½''×6½''	13½''×6½''	20½''×6½''
Appliqué Edge Orientation	right	left	right	left	right	left	right	left
Bottom Background Rectangle	30½''×6½''	24½''×6½''	6½''×6½''	16½''×6½''	25½''×6½''	15½''×6½''	19½''×6½''	12½''×6½''

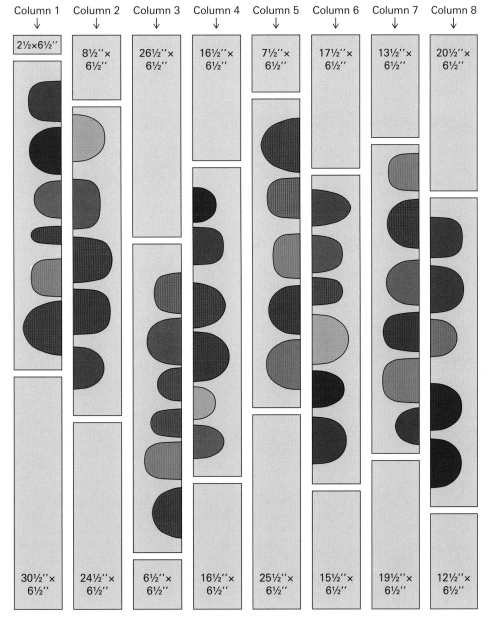

Column 1 → | Column 2 → | Column 3 → | Column 4 → | Column 5 → | Column 6 → | Column 7 → | Column 8 →

2½×6½'' | 8½''× 6½'' | 26½''× 6½'' | 16½''× 6½'' | 7½''× 6½'' | 17½''× 6½'' | 13½''× 6½'' | 20½''× 6½''

30½''× 6½'' | 24½''× 6½'' | 6½''× 6½'' | 16½''× 6½'' | 25½''× 6½'' | 15½''× 6½'' | 19½''× 6½'' | 12½''× 6½''

Figure 5.

ASSEMBLING THE BORDER STRIPS

1 Sew two strips of 4½"xWOF background fabric together along their short edges. Press open.

2 Trim the strip to 72½" in length.

3 Repeat with the other two 4½"xWOF strips.

ASSEMBLING THE QUILT TOP

1 Referencing Figure 6, sew the columns together along their long edges, beginning with column 1 on the left.

2 Attach the 4½"x72½" border strips on the right and left sides of the joined columns.

FINISHING

1 Layer the top with backing and batting, baste and quilt as desired.

2 Attach the binding using your favorite method.

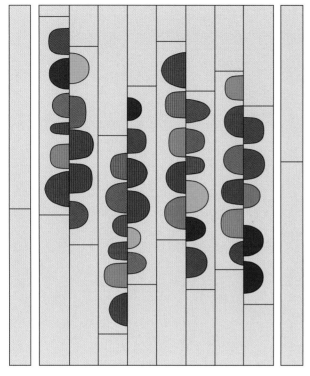

Figure 6.

From Alex Ledgerwood

One of my favorite quilters for scrap inspiration is Jolene Klaussen with her blog Blue Elephant Stitches. I love her improv quilts, as well as those she makes that follow a pattern. Her unique color sense and skill at coordinating disparate fabrics makes every quilt an example of her distinctive style. That isn't easy to do with scraps! Take a closer look at her work to learn more about using scraps in a way that expresses your own unique voice. Find her work at: blueelephantstitches.blogspot.com

LETTERPRESS

There is never a shortage of small strips in my scrap bin, and when the bin starts to overflow I love putting them to good use with a quick and easy pattern. The simple blocks of this quilt do a great job of showing off the scrap strips. The solid color and the white background fabrics balance out the scraps and give it a clean, modern look. Try using a bold solid color that coordinates with your scrap strips, but isn't too similar in color so that the block centers really stand out.

By Allison Harris

Finished Block Size: 6½″×9½″

Finished Quilt Size: 59″×76½″

MATERIALS

*Note: I've supplied two different piecing methods based on the kinds of scraps you may have. Gather the corresponding materials below, based on the chosen Assembly method for the Stacked Strip Sets (see page 25)

Scraps: If using the Strip Assembly, cut 24 strips 2"×WOF, and 16 strips 1½"×WOF

If using the Scrap Assembly, cut (216) 2"×4" rectangles and (144) 1½"×4" rectangles

Teal Solid Fabric: 1¾ yards

White Fabric: 1¾ yards

Binding Fabric: ⅝ yard

Backing Fabric: 4 yards

Batting: 67"×84"

CUTTING

*Note: Width of Fabric = WOF

From Teal Solid Fabric, cut:
- (29) 2"×WOF strips
  - Subcut each strip into (5) 2"×7" rectangles for a total of 144

From White Fabric, cut:
- (29) 2"×WOF strips
  - Subcut each strip into (5) 2"×7" rectangles for a total of 144

From Binding Fabric, cut:
- (8) 2½"×WOF strips

PIECING THE BLOCK UNITS

Depending on whether you use scraps or WOF strips, select the corresponding assembly technique.

Piecing the Stacked Strip Sets

Strip Assembly

1 Arrange (3) 2"×WOF print strips, and (2) 1½"×WOF print strips into rows. Alternate the strip widths, or arrange them as desired. Varying the order of strip layout will give the quilt a more improvisational look.

2 Sew the strips right sides together to form a strip set. Press seams open, or to either side. The assembled strip set should measure 7"×WOF.

3 Repeat Steps 1–2 to make a total of eight strip sets.

4 Cut each strip set into (9) 4"×7" units to create a total of 72 stacked strip set units measuring 4"×7". (Fig. 1)

Scrap Assembly

1 Arrange (3) 2"×4" print rectangles, and (2) 1½"×4" print rectangles into rows. Alternate the strips, or arrange them as desired. Varying the order of strip layout will give the quilt a more improvisational look.

2 Sew the rectangles right sides together along the 4" side to form a 4"×7" block. Press the seams open or to one side.

3 Repeat Steps 1–2 to create a total of 72 stacked strip set units.

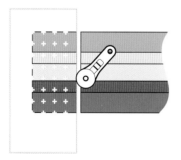

Figure 1.

Piecing A Block and B Block

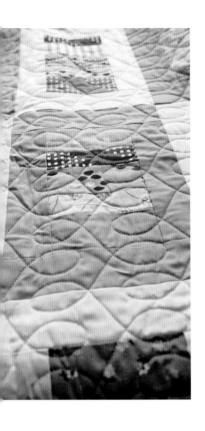

1 Place a teal 2"×7" rectangle on the 7" sides of a stacked strip set unit, right sides together. Sew and press the seams toward the teal rectangles. Sew a 2"×7" teal rectangle to the top and bottom of the block, pressing the seams toward the teal rectangles. The block should measure 7"×10".

2 Repeat Step 1 to create a total of 36 A Blocks with the teal borders, using a variety of different fabric stacked strip set unit combinations.

3 Using the remaining stacked strip set units, repeat Steps 1–2 using white 2"×7" rectangles to create a total of 36 B Blocks with white borders.

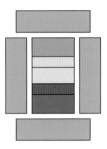

A Block: Make 36

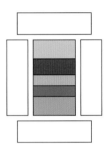

B Block: Make 36

INSPIRED SCRAPS From Allison Harris

Whenever I need some "scrap inspiration", I visit Bonnie Hunter's website, Quiltville (quiltville.com). It is full of great scrappy patterns, blocks and ideas. I've made her Dancing Nine's pattern, the Fun with Bricks quilt, plus a few other blocks that she has featured on her blog over the years. Her free patterns have great step-by-step photos and many of Bonnie's online tutorials have printer-friendly versions that you can download and keep as a handy reference. Next time you are in a scrap rut, browse through her long list of scrap friendly patterns and prepare to be inspired!

ASSEMBLING THE QUILT TOP

1 Referencing Figure 4, arrange the blocks into 8 rows of 9 blocks each, alternating between A Blocks and B Blocks.

2 Sew the blocks right sides together to form rows, pressing the seams towards the teal blocks. Sew the rows together, pressing the seams to one side to finish the quilt top.

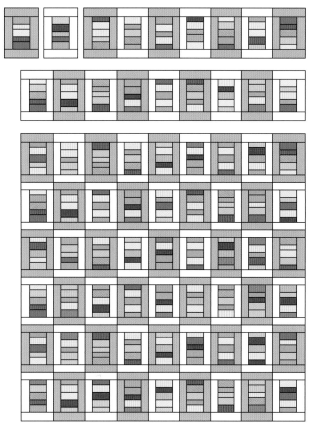

Figure 4.

FINISHING

1 Layer the quilt top with backing and batting, baste and quilt as desired.

2 Attach the binding using your favorite method.

FLETCHING

By Amy Friend

This design is based on a highly simplified, stylized interpretation of the fletchings, or feathers, at the end of an arrow. Each block is paper pieced using 2½'' strips from your scrap bin to represent the arrow with two pairs of feathers. Most of the blocks are made with two fabric choices; one for the arrow and one pair of fletchings and another fabric for the remaining two fletchings. But the fabric placement is changed up a bit in some of the blocks, to draw your eye away from the block based design. Mixing it up keeps your eye moving over the quilt, searching for the pattern. There are so many possible layouts using this block. Because this quilt design calls for 2½'' strips, it's also jelly roll friendly!

Finished Block Size: 12''x12''

Finished Quilt Size: 60''x72''

MATERIALS

Fabric A: assorted 2½'' wide scraps in mint green, jade, peach, coral, soft pink, pink, light blue, medium gray-blue, dove gray

Fabric B: 4 yards mint green solid

Binding Fabric: ½ yard

Backing Fabric: 4¼ yards

Batting: 68''×80''

Foundation paper

Acrylic ruler

CUTTING

Note: Width of Fabric = WOF

From Fabric A, cut:
- (120) 2½''×9'' strips
- (30) 2½''×13'' strips

From Fabric B, cut:
- (60) 2½''×9'' strips
- (60) 6½''×10'' rectangles
  - Referencing the Cutting Diagrams, mark each rectangle and divide into two stacks of 30.
    Note: If you are using a solid background fabric like I did, you can just make 60 using Diagram A and simply invert each cut as necessary.

From Binding, cut:
- (7) 2½''×WOF strips

Cutting Diagrams for the (60) 6½''×10'' rectangles

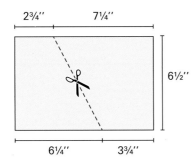

Cutting Diagram A: Make 30

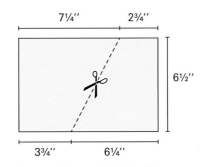

Cutting Diagram B: Make 30

PREPARATION

1 Print 30 copies of the Templates A and B (see page 118) onto your favorite foundation paper.

2 Referencing the Block Diagrams, consider your fabric placement and mark each pattern piece with the desired colors before you begin to sew.

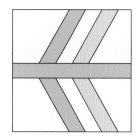

Block Diagram 1

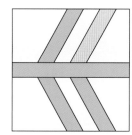

Block Diagram 2

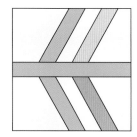

Block Diagram 3

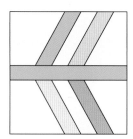

Block Diagram 4

INSPIRED SCRAPS **From Amy Friend**

Ayumi Takahashi masterfully uses every little scrap to create wonderfully appealing projects. She kindly offers a number of them on her blog as free tutorials including a paper pieced Teapot block, a Tissue Box Cover and Fabric Basket, all of which I have made! I added a paper pieced teacup to the Teapot Block to make a pillow for my mother. The fabric basket was the first of Ayumi's tutorials that I tried quite a few years ago now. Ayumi is the author of *Patchwork Please!*, a book loaded with scrappy Zakka projects and the blog Pink Penguin.

PIECING THE BLOCK

1 If paper piecing is new to you, consult the instructions on page 11. Sew the pieces together, following the order indicated on the numbered template. Use the smaller subcut background fabric pieces for section A5 and the larger subcut background fabric pieces for section A1.

2 Continue using this method to sew pieces in the order indicated on the template.

3 Position the block fabric side down and using your ruler, trim the block to include a ¼'' seam allowance. Carefully remove the paper template from the block.

4 Repeat until you have completed 30 A Templates.

5 Repeat Steps 1–4 to complete 30 B Templates. Use the smaller subcut background fabric pieces for section B1 and the larger subcut background fabric pieces for section B5.

6 Pair the Templates A and B with right sides facing and stitch the blocks together. Do not press the blocks open yet. Create 30 completed blocks.

QUILTER TO QUILTER

- - - - - - - - - - - - - - - - - - - -

For foundation piecing, reduce your stitch length to about 1.7mm and use a size 90 needle for ease of paper removal.

ASSEMBLING THE QUILT TOP

1 Referring to Figure 1, arrange your blocks into 6 rows of 5 blocks each.

2 Starting at the upper left corner, join the blocks into rows. Press the seams of adjoining blocks so that they will nest whenever possible. Press seams of row 1 and all odd numbered rows to the left. Press seams of even numbered rows to the right.

3 Sew the rows together nesting the seams. Press.

Figure 1.

FINISHING

1 Layer the top with backing and batting, baste and quilt as desired.

2 Attach the binding using your favorite method.

SCRAP BAG STARS

One of my favorite things about creating with scraps is that it gives me a chance to play with a variety of different color combinations that I may have never tried before. For this quilt I wanted to pull together colors that made me think of summer—sky blues, sunny golds, corals, and warm oranges.

Scrap Bag Stars is a great way to use up lots of those skinny string scraps that seem to accumulate easily. Or you can just cut strips of varying widths off the ends of fabric in your stash. A variety of different widths will give the quilt added interest, but I stick to skinnier strips to make it most interesting. Sewing these strips into panels gives the quilt an added depth and design element. This look would work with monochromatic scraps or a full color spectrum.

By Amy Smart

Quilted by Melissa Kelley

Finished Block Size: 9''x9''

Finished Quilt Size: 72''x72''

MATERIALS

Scraps: An assortment of scraps in aqua blues, golds, pinks and corals.

White Fabric: 3 yards or 40 white pre-cut squares 10''×10''

Binding Fabric: ⅝ yard

Backing Fabric: 4½ yards

Batting: 80''×80''

QUILTER TO QUILTER

To save time, you might want to get a stack of pre-cut 10'' white squares. I used Moda Bella Solids that come 42 to a bundle.

CUTTING

Note: Width of Fabric = WOF

From Blue, Gold, Pink, and Coral Scraps, cut:
- (48) 5'' squares
- A large assortment of strips 10½''–11'' long and varying widths of 1½''–2½''

From White Fabric (if not using pre-cuts), cut:
- (24) 10'' squares
- (16) 9½'' squares

From Binding Fabric, cut:
- (8) 2½''×WOF strips OR 300'' continuous bias binding.

Bonus scrap quilt!

Save the triangles you trim from each A and C Block (Fig. 2). Keep them in a stack and then chain piece them together all at once along the long edge of the triangles. This will give you 48 half-square triangle blocks all ready to sew together in a cute mini quilt or to use as part of a pieced backing!

ASSEMBLING THE BLOCKS

A Blocks

1 Draw a diagonal line on the wrong side of all of the 5″ squares.

2 Position a marked 5″ square in the corner of a white 9½″ square, right sides together (Fig. 1). Sew on the drawn line.

3 Trim excess fabric leaving a ¼″ seam allowance (Fig. 2). Press seam away from the white fabric.

4 Repeat Steps 2–3 to create a total of 16 A Blocks.

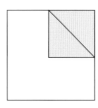

Figure 1.

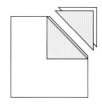

Figure 2.

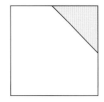

A Blocks: Make 16

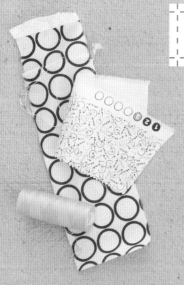

INSPIRED SCRAPS From Amy Smart

One of my favorite sources of inspiration for using scraps is Amanda Jean Nyberg, author of the popular blog, Crazy Mom Quilts. No scrap is too small for Amanda Jean! As a result, I love the book she co-authored with Cheryl Arkison, *Sunday Morning Quilts*. There are so many great projects and ideas in that book for playing with your favorite scraps as well as patterns to create some stunning quilts. It's an equally great resource for ideas for sorting and storing your favorite scraps.

B and C Blocks

1 Sew 6–7 assorted 10½'' strips together along the long sides to create a scrappy strip set about 10½'' square (Fig. 3). Repeat to create a total of 24 sets.

2 Draw a diagonal line on the wrong side of 24 white 10'' squares. Center each white square on top of one of a strip set and sew a ¼'' away from either side of the drawn line. (Fig. 4)

3 Carefully cut on the drawn line to create two half-square triangle blocks. Repeat to create a total of 48 half square triangle blocks. Press the seams toward the white.

4 Trim each block to 9½'' square.

5 Set aside 16 of these blocks. These are your B Blocks.

6 Position the remaining (32) 5'' squares on the white corner of the half square triangle block, right sides together.

7 Sew on the drawn line and trim away excess fabric ¼'' from the seam. Press seam toward the 5'' triangle.

8 Repeat to create a total of 32 C Blocks.

QUILTER TO QUILTER

A wide variety of string widths will make this project interesting and give some texture to the design.

Figure 3.

Figure 4.

IMPORTANT

Make sure that your diagonal line goes in the same direction across the pieced strips on ALL blocks. (For example from top-left to bottom-right.) This will make the strips go in contrasting directions when you arrange your quilt blocks.

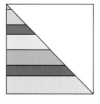
B Blocks: Make 16

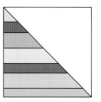
Remaining half-square triangle units for C Blocks: 32

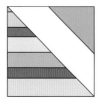
C Blocks: Make 32

ASSEMBLING THE QUILT

1 Referencing Figure 5 for block placement, arrange 8 rows of 8 blocks each.

2 Sew the blocks into eight rows. Press the seams all in one direction, alternating directions on alternating rows (i.e. all seams to the left on odd rows and to the right on even rows.)

3 Sew the rows together and press the seams in one direction.

FINISHING

1 Layer the top with backing and batting, baste and quilt as desired.

2 Attach the binding using your favorite method.

Figure 5.

Made with
SQUARES

SQUARE-RIFIC!

By April Rosenthal

It's no secret that I'm obsessed with tiny squares of fabric. I swoon at the sight of classic postage stamp quilts and am completely smitten with those adorable 2½'' square pre-cuts. Square-Rific! is my tribute to all those lovely little squares, in an awesome throw quilt that is sure to have you using up your pre-cut leftovers and showing off your fantastic quilt to anyone who will stand still long enough to look at it!

Finished Block Size: 12''x12''

Finished Quilt Size: 60½''x72½''

MATERIALS

Scraps: Assortment of scraps totaling approximately 4½ yards

Scraps: Assortment of white/low-volume scraps at least 14" wide, totaling approximately 2 yards

Backing: 4 yards

Binding: ½ yard

Batting: 67"×79"

CUTTING

Note: Width of Fabric = WOF

From Assorted Scraps, cut:
- (540) 2½" squares
- (630) 2" squares

From White Scraps, cut:
- (15) 13½" squares
  - Subcut each square diagonally for a total of 30 triangles

From Binding, cut:
- (7) 2½"×WOF strips

Shortcut

If you have 2½" pre-cut strips you'd like to use for this project, take this shortcut! Instead of cutting (540) 2½" squares, use 36 WOF strips. Sew strips together lengthwise, in sets of 6 strips. Press seams to one side. Square up the edge, and cut (16) 2½" segments crosswise from each set. Continue with the pattern as directed, beginning at Step 2 of A Block assembly.

ASSEMBLING A BLOCKS

1 Stitch together 2½'' squares, into rows of six. Press all seams to one side. Each row should measure 2½''×12½''.

2 Assemble the block by sewing six rows together, rotating the pressed strips so that the seams nest.

3 Repeat Steps 1–2 to create a total of 15 A Blocks.

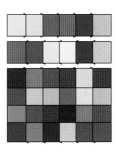

A Block: Make 15

ASSEMBLING B BLOCKS

1 Stitch together (6) 2'' squares to make a row. Repeat to create a total of (30) 6-Patch rows. Press seams to one side. (Fig. 1)

2 Stitch together (5) 2'' squares to make a row. Repeat to create a total of (30) 5-Patch rows. Press seams to one side. (Fig. 2)

3 Stitch together (4) 2'' squares to make a row. Repeat to create a total of (30) 4-Patch rows. Press seams to one side. (Fig. 3)

4 Stitch together (3) 2'' squares to make a row. Repeat to create a total of (30) 3-Patch rows. Press seams to one side. (Fig. 4)

5 Stitch together (2) 2'' squares to make a row. Repeat to create a total of (30) 2-Patch rows. Press seams to one side. (Fig. 5)

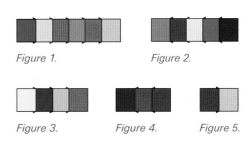

Figure 1.   *Figure 2.*

Figure 3.   *Figure 4.*   *Figure 5.*

6 Stitch row units together in decreasing order, keeping the bottom blocks of each row aligned along the raw edge and rotating strips so that the seams nest. Beginning with a 6-Patch row, stitch to a 5-Patch row to one side. Sew a 4-Patch row to the 5-Patch row. Sew a 3-Patch row to the 4-Patch row. Sew a 2-Patch row to the 3-Patch row. Stitch a single square to the 2-Patch row. Press all seams toward the right side. Repeat to create 30 patchwork units. (Fig. 6)

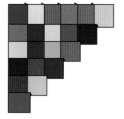

Figure 6.

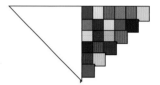

Figure 7.

7 Sew one patchwork unit to one white triangle. Press toward the triangle. (Fig. 7)

8 Sew two triangle units together to make the B Block, nesting seams at the center. Trim to 12½", being sure to leave ¼" beyond the patchwork intersections.

9 Repeat to create a total of 15 B Blocks.

B Blocks: Make 15

ASSEMBLING THE QUILT

1 Referencing Figure 8, arrange blocks in an alternating pattern, 5 blocks in each row, beginning with a B Block. Assemble 6 rows, 3 beginning and ending with B Blocks, and 3 beginning and ending with A Blocks. Press seams toward the A Blocks. Stitch rows together carefully—don't stretch those bias edges on the B Blocks! Press.

FINISHING

1 Layer the top with backing and batting, baste and quilt as desired.

2 Attach the binding using your favorite method.

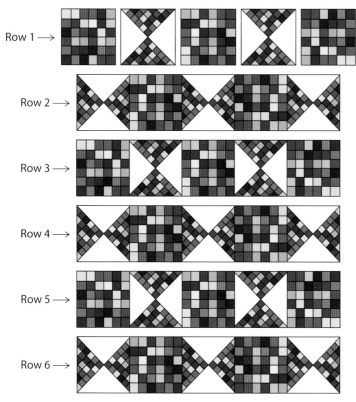

Row 1 →

Row 2 →

Row 3 →

Row 4 →

Row 5 →

Row 6 →

Figure 8.

QUILTER TO QUILTER

Secure those small pieces and bias edges by stitching all the way around the outer edge of your quilt with a short baste stitch and a ⅛'' seam allowance. This will help your quilt stay intact and avoid distortion while your quilt is quilted. The seam doesn't need to be removed, as it will be covered by binding.

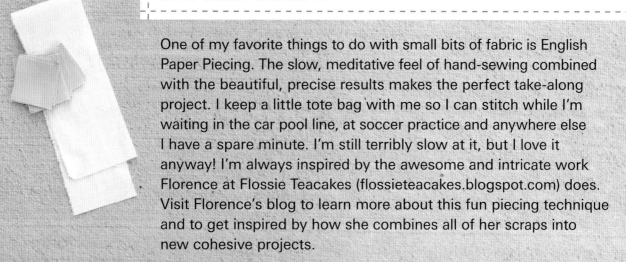

INSPIRED SCRAPS From April Rosenthal

One of my favorite things to do with small bits of fabric is English Paper Piecing. The slow, meditative feel of hand-sewing combined with the beautiful, precise results makes the perfect take-along project. I keep a little tote bag with me so I can stitch while I'm waiting in the car pool line, at soccer practice and anywhere else I have a spare minute. I'm still terribly slow at it, but I love it anyway! I'm always inspired by the awesome and intricate work Florence at Flossie Teacakes (flossieteacakes.blogspot.com) does. Visit Florence's blog to learn more about this fun piecing technique and to get inspired by how she combines all of her scraps into new cohesive projects.

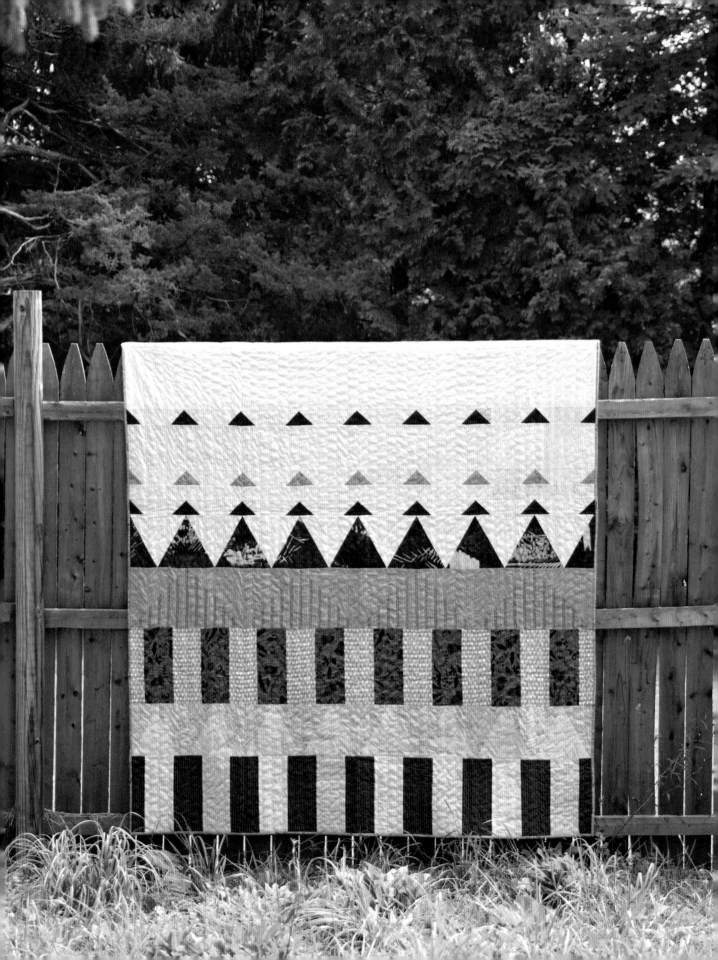

Made with
STRIPS

CHIMNEY SWIFTS

By Dorie Schwarz

I love making row quilts because I like watching patterns emerge and change as I stack simple shapes on top of each other. There is a lot of room for play with contrast and color in row quilts. This quilt builds from straight lines and lower contrast into triangles and higher contrast. The overall effect reminds me of the chimney swifts that flutter over our rooftop during the summer—the dark triangles are the birds and the other layers are the buildings. This quilt uses bigger fabric scraps, and it would be good for using up the oddly shaped pieces left over from cutting out garment sewing projects.

Finished Quilt Size: 64"×85"

MATERIALS

For all fabric requirements, use an equal amount of scrap fabrics for the yardage listed

Dark Gray Fabric and Light Gray Fabric (row 1): ½ yard each

Dark Blue Fabric (rows 2, 10): ½ yard

Dark Teal Fabric (rows 3, 5, 9): ¼ yard

Pond Green Fabric (row 7): ¼ yard

Off-White Fabric (plus assorted low volume scraps, if desired) **(rows 2–10):** 2½ yards

Light Blue Print Fabric (row 11): ⅔ yard

Light Gray Fabric (row 11): ⅔ yard

Dark Blue and Light Gold Fabric (row 12): ½ yard each

Light Blue and Pink Fabric (row 13): ½ yard each

Dark Blue Fabric and Beige Fabric (row 14): ½ yard each

Backing Fabric: ¼ yard

Binding Fabric: ¾ yard

Batting: 72"×93"

QUILTER TO QUILTER

The directional fabric used in the large flying geese row has a loose weave. This type of fabric will be more durable if a light interfacing is applied to the back of the fabric before sewing.

INSPIRED SCRAPS From Dorie Schwarz

Lynn Carson Harris is my biggest scrap inspiration. I have had the pleasure of getting to know Lynn through our MQG, and I remember trying to tone down my awe the first time I saw one of her projects in person. She is such a skilled quilter, and, unlike my project in this book, she works with very small pieces. Lynn believes in using *Every Last Piece*, and fittingly that is the name of her book. Her Stardust quilt in that book is particularly stunning—it inspires me to reach for the (tiny) stars! Lynn blogs at thelittleredhen.typepad.com.

CUTTING

Note: Width of Fabric = WOF

Cutting Chart

Row	Type	Color A	Color B
1	rectangle	light gray	dark gray
2, 10	equilateral triangle	off-white	dark blue
3, 5, 9	flying geese	off-white	dark teal
4	solid	off-white (10½'')	
6	solid	off-white (6½'')	
7	flying geese	off-white	pond green
8	solid	off-white (2½'')	
11	large flying geese	light blue	light gray
12	rectangle	dark blue	gold
13	equilateral triangle	light blue	pink
14	rectangle	beige	dark blue

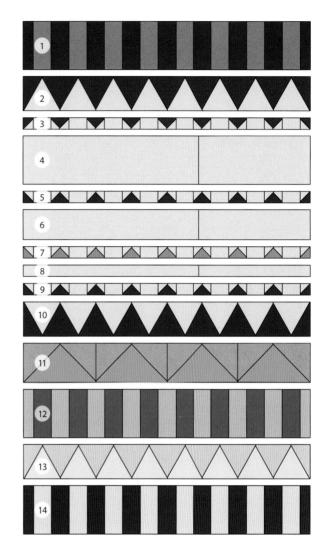

From Binding Fabric, cut:
- (8) 2½''×WOF strips

Rectangles
Rows 1, 12 and 14

From Color A, cut:
- (1) 10½''×WOF strip
  - Subcut into (8) 4½'' rectangles

From Color B, cut:
- (1) 10½''×WOF strip
  - Subcut (7) 4½'' rectangles and (2) 2½'' rectangles

Equilateral Triangles
Rows 2, 10 and 13

For each of the rows labeled "equilateral triangle" in the Cutting Chart:

From Color A, cut:
- (8) triangles using the Full Triangle Template (see page 119)

From Color B, cut:
- (7) triangles using the Full Triangle Template (see page 119)
- (2) half-triangles using the Half Triangle Template. Note: cut one of the template and one of the template reversed (see page 119)

Flying Geese
Rows 3, 5, 7, 9 and 11

For each of the rows labeled "flying geese" in the Cutting Chart:

From Color A, cut:
- (2) 2½"×WOF strips
  - Subcut (1) 3" square, (14) 2½" squares and (8) 2½"×4½" rectangles

From Color B, cut:
- (1) 3"×WOF strip
  - Subcut (1) 3" square and (7) 2½"×4½" rectangles from the remainder

Solid Rows
Rows 4, 6 and 8

For the rows labeled "solid" in the Cutting Chart, cut:

- (2) 10½"xWOF strips
- (2) 6½"xWOF strips
- (2) 2½"xWOF strips

Large Flying Geese

For each of the rows labeled "large flying geese" in the Cutting Chart:

From Color A, cut:
- (2) 8½"x WOF strips
  - Subcut (4) 8½" x 16½" rectangles

From Color B, cut:
- (2) 8½"x WOF strips
  - Subcut (8) 8½" squares

*Note: If you are using directional prints and want all of the prints to be oriented in the same direction, you will have to cut twice the number of pieces indicated in the cutting instructions. This will yield extra flying geese units, so consider incorporating them into a pieced backing.

ASSEMBLING THE ROWS

Rectangle Rows

1 Sew Color A and Color B rectangles together along the 10½'' sides, beginning and ending with a 2½'' wide Color B rectangle, as shown in the Quilt Assembly Diagram. Press seams open or to one side.

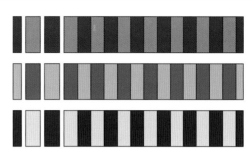

Figure 1: Rectangle rows.

Equilateral Triangle Rows

1 Align one Color A triangle with one Color B triangle, right sides together. Sew along one side. Press seams to the darker fabric. Repeat with the remaining triangles, and sew the pairs into a row, adding the remaining Color A triangle to the end. Sew the Color B half-triangles to each end of the rows.

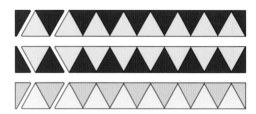

Figure 2: Equilateral triangle rows.

Flying Geese Rows

1 Using 14 Color A squares and 7 Color B rectangles, create 7 flying geese units (see page 9) per row.

2 Pair together one Color A and one Color B 3'' square. Create two HST units (see page 9) per row.

3 Referencing Figure 3, sew the rows together, placing one flying geese unit between each 4½'' Color A rectangle. Sew one HST unit to each end. Press all seams to the darker fabric.

Figure 3: Flying geese rows.

Large Flying Geese Row

1 Using 4 Color A rectangles and 8 Color B squares, create (4) 16½"×8½" Large flying geese units (see page 9).

2 Press to the darker fabric.

3 Referencing Figure 4, sew the row together along the short sides of the blocks. Press seams open.

Solid Rows

1 Trim the selvage from each WOF strip. Sew the solid fabric cuts together along the short sides. Trim so that each of the three solid pieces is 64½" long.

*Note: If you are mixing in other low volume prints, consider making the cuts 4½" (or multiples of 4 plus ½") wide so that they line up with the rows of the quilt.

Figure 4: Large flying geese row.

ASSEMBLING THE QUILT TOP

1 Referencing Figure 5, arrange the pieced strips into rows. Pin rows right sides together into groups of two, matching seams and points. Sew rows together, then repeat with groups of four, etc., until the quilt top is complete. Press.

FINISHING

1 Layer the top with backing and batting, baste and quilt as desired.

2 Attach the binding using your favorite method.

Figure 5.

ARGYLE MEDALLION

By Erin Burke Harris

Quilted by Natalia Bonner

I love taking traditional quilting elements and updating them into something fun and unexpected. The variety of shapes and the on-point setting make this medallion anything but ordinary. The design is reminiscent of a traditional argyle pattern, but I chose to use more modern fabric scraps inspired by my early summer garden, awash with blooming peonies and hydrangeas. But don't feel that you need to limit your palette to a few hues as I did! This quilt is a great opportunity to play with scraps and color to create your very own argyle. I can imagine these spinning Dresden blade circles and simple patchwork borders in a riot of color as well as in more monochromatic tones. Any way you chose to make it, it's sure to be fun!

Finished Quilt Size: 78"x78"

MATERIALS

Dresden Blade Scraps: (40) 5″×3½″ and (40) 6½″×3½″ bright colored scraps (lime, aqua, magenta, green and pink)

Dresden Center Scraps: 4 navy scraps at least 5″ square

9-Patch Block Scraps: 32 navy scraps at least 2½″×10½″ (approximately ⅝ yard) and 32 low-volume/light background scraps at least 2½″×10½″ (approximately ⅝ yard)

Flying Geese Scraps: 48 low volume/light background scraps at least 6½″×3½″ (approximately ¾ yard) and 96 bright colored scraps at least 3½″ square (approximately 1 yard)

Square-in-Square Block Scraps: 4 magenta scraps at least 3½″ square (approximately ⅛ yard), 16 aqua scraps at least 3½″ square (approximately ⅛ yard) and 5 lime scraps at least 6½″ square (approximately ¼ yard)

Background Fabric: 4 yards

Backing Fabric: 7½ yards

Binding Fabric: ¾ yard

Batting: 86″×86″

Aluminum Foil: 4 pieces approximately 6″ square

Water-soluble marker

Card stock

Spray starch

Acrylic ruler

CUTTING

Note: Width of Fabric = WOF

From Dresden Blade Scraps, cut:
- (40) 5″×3½″ rectangles
- (40) 6½″×3½″ rectangles

From Center Circle Scraps, cut:
- (4) 5″ squares from navy fabric

From 9-Patch Scraps, cut:
- (32) 2½″×10½″ rectangles from navy fabrics
- (32) 2½″×10½″ rectangles from low-volume/light background fabrics

From Flying Geese Scraps, cut:
- (48) 6½″×3½″ rectangles from low-volume/light background fabrics
- (96) 3½″ squares from bright fabrics

From Square-in-Square Scraps, cut:
- (5) 6½″ squares from lime green fabrics
- (4) 3½″ squares from magenta fabrics
- (16) 3½″ squares from aqua fabrics

From Background Fabric, cut:
- 16 Quarter Arches using Template (see page 121)
- (4) 25″ squares
Before subcutting, spray the 25″ squares with spray starch. This helps prevent stretching along the long bias edge once it is cut.
  - Sub-cut in half diagonally to yield 8 half-square triangles
- (40) 2″×3½″ rectangles
- (8) 2½″×10½″ rectangles
- (2) 5⅛″ squares
  - Sub-cut in half diagonally to yield 4 half-square triangles

From Binding Fabric, cut:
- (9) 2½″×WOF strips

PIECING THE CIRCLE BLOCKS

1 Sew each 2''x3½'' background rectangle to a corresponding 5''x3½'' dresden blade scrap along the 3½'' side with right sides together. Press seams towards the background fabric. Repeat to create 40 pieced units.

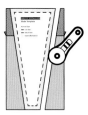

Figure 1.

2 Align the Blade Template (see page 120) with the top background fabric edge of the 40 pieced blades and trim along the template sides (Fig. 1). Repeat with the (40) 6½''x3½'' rectangles.

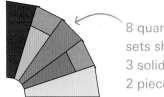

Figure 2.

8 quarter circle sets should have 3 solid blades and 2 pieced blades.

3 Referencing Figures 2 and 3, arrange blades in sets of 5, alternating a solid blade with a pieced blade. Beginning at the longer, outer edge and with right sides together, sew the blades to one another. Press the seams in one direction. Repeat to create a total of 16 quarter circles.

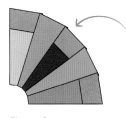

Figure 3.

The remaining 8 quarter circle sets should have 3 pieced blades and 2 solid blades.

4 Fold each quarter blade unit in half, right sides together, aligning the long edges. Finger press the fold at the outer edge to mark the center and unfold.

QUILTER TO QUILTER

Take your time while making the circle blocks. Because the center of the block is an open circle, it is best to arrange the blocks on a flat surface and pin them together while flat before sewing them so everything lines up properly. You may find that using a spray starch will help keep the curved and bias edges from distorting as will sewing all the seams from the outside edges towards the center. Finally, before sewing, double check that the pieced and solid blades alternate to avoid unnecessary seam ripping.

5 Fold each quarter arch unit in half, right sides together, aligning straight edges and ends. Finger press the fold at the inner edge of the arch to mark the center.

6 With right sides together and aligning the raw edges, pin the finger pressed center mark of the quarter arch unit to the corresponding center mark of the quarter blade unit. Pin each quarter arch side edge to the corresponding quarter blade side edge. Ease the fabric between the center and the sides, pinning in place. Sew together using a ¼'' seam. (Figs. 4–5)

7 With right sides together, sew each quarter circle block that has solid blades on its side edges to a corresponding quarter circle block that has pieced blades on its side edges to yield 8 half circle blocks. Take care to ensure that each pair is sewn identically. Press all the seams in the same direction.

8 Sew the half circle blocks together to create a total of 4 circle blocks (Fig. 6). Press the seams open.

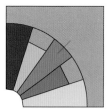

Figure 4. *Figure 5.*

Note: *In order to have nesting seams, press the seams of the sets with pieced blades on the edges towards the blades and press the seams of the sets with the solid blades on the edges towards the arch.*

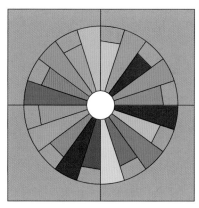

Figure 6.

Attaching the Center Circles

1 Using the card stock, trace and cut the circle template (see page 121). Center the template on a 5" navy square and pin into place. Using a water-soluble pen, trace around the circle, ½" away from the template. Remove the template and cut along the drawn line (Fig. 7). Repeat to create a total of 4 center circles.

2 Place a center circle right side down on a piece of aluminum foil and position the card stock template centered on top (Fig. 8). Fold the aluminum foil and fabric up over the edges of the template, little by little, smoothing out any wrinkles as you work (Fig. 9). Using a hot iron, carefully press the edges all around the circle (Fig. 10). Position the circle with the foil right side up and give the circle a final press. Wait for the foil to cool, then carefully peel the foil away from the fabric (Fig. 11). Remove the card stock template. Repeat to create a total of 4 turned-edge center circles (Fig. 12).

3 Position a circle block on a flat surface and center the turned center circle over the center hole. The appliqué should overlap the raw edges of the hole by about ½". Pin or baste the center circle in place and use your favorite method to attach the appliqué to the circle block. Repeat to create a total of 4 completed circle blocks. (Fig. 13)

Figure 7.

Figure 8.

Figure 9.

Figure 10.

Figure 11.

Figure 12.

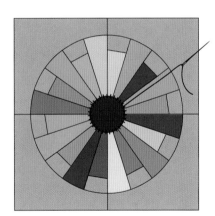

Figure 13.

QUILTER TO QUILTER

I chose to needle-turn appliqué the center circles to the circle blocks, but you could machine stitch the appliqué instead. Skipping Step 2 of turning under the edges of the circle appliqué and leaving a raw edge would create a different effect too.

PIECING THE 9-PATCH ROWS

1 With right sides together, sew a
2½"×10½" navy strip to each side
of a 2½"×10½" background strip
along the 10½" side. Press the
seams towards the navy. The unit
will measure 6½"×10½". Repeat
to create a total of 8 A sets.

2 With right sides together, sew a
2½"×10½" low volume/light background rectangle to each side of a
2½"×10½" navy rectangle along the
10½" side. Press the seam towards
the navy. The set will measure
6½"×10½". Repeat 15 additional
times for a total of 16 B strips.

3 Using a rotary cutter and a ruler,
subcut each A strip set into (4)
2½"×6½" units (Fig. 14) to create
a total of 32 subcut A units. (Note
that the sets are a ½" longer than
needed to allow for squaring up the
ends if necessary.) Repeat with each
B strip set (Fig. 15) to create a total
of 64 subcut B units.

4 Referencing Figure 16, sew the strips
together along the 6½" side. Press the
seam towards the B strips. Repeat to
create a total of (32) 9-Patch blocks.

5 Sew the 9-Patch blocks into 8 rows
of 4 blocks each. Press the seams
in one direction.

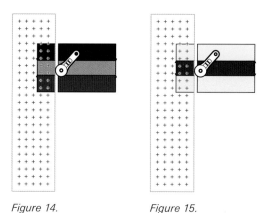

Figure 14.   Figure 15.

Figure 16.

9-Patch Rows: Make 8

Figure 17.

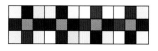

Flying Geese Rows: Make 8

Figure 18.   Figure 19.   Figure 20.   Square-in-a-Square Blocks

PIECING THE FLYING GEESE ROWS

1 See page 9 for instructions on creating the flying geese units. Gather the 6½''×3½'' rectangles from low-volume/light background fabrics and the 3½'' squares from the brights.

2 Create a total of 48 flying geese units. (Fig. 17)

3 Sew the flying geese units into 8 rows of 6 units each. Press the seams in one direction.

PIECING THE SQUARE-IN-A-SQUARE BLOCKS

1 Mark a diagonal line from corner to corner on the wrong side of (4) 3½'' magenta squares. With right sides together, place (2) 3½'' magenta squares on top of (1) 6½'' lime square, matching raw edges, and ensuring that the drawn line runs from the center of one side of the lime square to the center of a second side (Fig. 18). Sew on the drawn lines and trim the corners ¼'' from the sewn line (Fig. 19). Press.

2 Repeat for the remaining two corners using the remaining (2) 3½'' magenta squares. (Fig. 20)

3 Make four additional square-in-a-square blocks using the same method and the remaining 6½'' lime squares and the (16) 3½'' aqua squares.

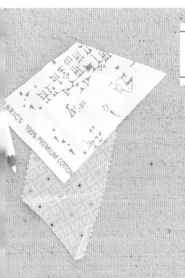

INSPIRED SCRAPS From Erin Burke Harris

My favorite way to use scraps is with improvisational piecing and I give all the credit to Denyse Schmidt's first book, *Quilts*. Her book inspired me to create a quilt in 2008 made entirely from orange scraps and white fabric. It sat unfinished until I revisited it in mid-2014. It was a treat to see scraps of my first favorite fabrics and to flashback to the hot summer when I pieced this quilt with my then little girls playing in the next room. I love how quilts can mark a moment in time.

ASSEMBLING THE QUILT TOP

1 Referencing Figure 21, arrange the circle blocks, (4) 9-Patch row units, flying geese rows and square-in-a-square blocks taking care that the flying geese rows are pointed in the correct direction.

2 Sew each block and row together pressing seams in one direction for rows 1 and 3 and the opposite direction for row 2. (Fig. 21)

3 Center the long diagonal end of a 5⅛" background half-square triangle on the end of (1) 9-Patch row and sew in place. Press the seam toward the triangle. Repeat with the remaining (3) 5⅛" background half-square triangles and (3) 9-patch rows to yield (4) 9-patch corner units.

4 Sew (1) 25" background half-square triangle to (1) 9-Patch corner unit along one of the large triangle's shorter sides, aligning the ends. Sew a second 25" background half-square triangle to the opposite side of the 9-patch corner unit. Press seams towards the background triangles. Repeat three times for a total of four corner triangle units.

5 Referencing Figure 23, attach a corner triangle unit to each edge of the center medallion, matching seams. Press.

Figure 21.

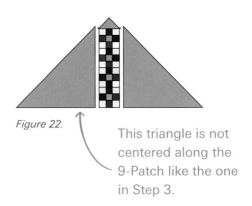

Figure 22.

This triangle is not centered along the 9-Patch like the one in Step 3.

Figure 23.

FINISHING

1 Layer the top with backing and batting, baste and quilt as desired.

2 Attach the binding using your favorite method.

SWEET EMMELINE

By Janice Zeller Ryan

Most of my favorite quilts are scrap quilts. I like to save even the tiniest pieces of special fabrics in the hopes of using them later, and use them I do! I love the texture and visual interest that is created by using a variety of patterns, colors and textures. My choice of scraps for Sweet Emmeline is more focused than my previous scrap quilts, as I grouped like colors together and then broke them down further into light and dark shades. You can definitely be more random with your scrap selections, but be sure you choose various values, so you have contrast in your piecing.

Finished Block Size: 8″×8″

Finished Quilt Size: 58″×78″

MATERIALS

Light and Dark Blue Scraps:
a variety to equal ⅔ yard

Light and Dark Orange Scraps:
a variety to equal ⅔ yard

Light and Dark Yellow Scraps:
a variety to equal ⅔ yard

Light and Dark Aqua Scraps:
a variety to equal ⅔ yard

Light and Dark Green Scraps:
a variety to equal ⅔ yard

Light and Dark Brown Scraps:
a variety to equal ⅔ yard

Light and Dark Pink Scraps:
a variety to equal ⅔ yard

Navy Blue (for star points): 1¼ yards

White Polka Dot Fabric: 4 yards

Gray Background Fabric: 6 yards

Binding Fabric: ½ yard

Backing Fabric: 5¼ yards

Batting: 66″×86″

Acrylic ruler

Template plastic

Copy paper

CUTTING

Note: Width of Fabric = WOF

From Scraps, cut (from EACH color):
- (14) 2¾″×3½″ rectangles
- (14) 2¾″×3¼″ rectangles
- (14) 2½″ squares

Note: *Once cut, group the above pieces into 48 sets. Each set is made up of two dark and two light rectangles of each size and two dark and two light squares.*

From Assorted Scraps, cut:
- (82) 3″×3½″ rectangles for sashing
- (35) 2½″ squares for star and block centers

Note: *Cut 18 matching sets of four rectangles each and 10 rectangles that are random colors.*

From Navy Blue, cut:
- (11) 3½″ strips
  - Subcut each strip into (16) 2½″×3½″ rectangles, for a total of 164 rectangles (for star points)

From White Polka Dot, cut:
- (10) 4¼″ strips
  - Subcut into (16) 2″×4¼″ rectangles, for a total of 192 rectangles
- (6) 3½″ strips
  - Subcut into (14) 3″×3½″ rectangles, for a total of 82 rectangles

QUILTER TO QUILTER

Since most of the pieces you are cutting will be used in paper piecing, save yourself some time and don't try to be exact with your cutting. The only pieces that need to be precise are the 2½″ star and block centers and the Template A background pieces.

From Gray Background Fabric, cut:

- 96 pieces from Template A using the plastic template created in Preparation and referencing Figure 1 for cutting placement
- (11) 3½'' strips
  - Subcut each strip into (16) 2½''×3½'' rectangles, for a total of 164 rectangles for sashing
- (4) 6½'' strips
  - Subcut each strip into (24) 1¾''×6½'' rectangles, for a total of 82 rectangles for sashing
- (4) 5¼'' strips
  - Subcut each strip into (24) 1¾''×5¼'' rectangles, for a total of 82 rectangles for sashing

From Binding Fabric, cut:

- (7) 2¼''×WOF strips

use these scraps for paper piecing

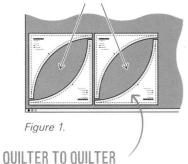

Figure 1.

QUILTER TO QUILTER

When cutting the Template A background pieces, invert the plastic template every other cut to maximize your yardage. Be sure to save those leaf-shaped scraps of fabric to use in other projects.

PREPARATION

Print the following number of templates at 100% (see pages 122–123):

- Template A: print 1 copy and trace onto template plastic.
- Template B: print 96 copies
- Template C: print 96 copies
- Template D: print 82 copies

PIECING TEMPLATES B AND C

1 Referencing Figure 2 and working in numerical order, paper-piece two of Template B using the following fabrics in each space:

- 1: Light Blue 2¾''×3½'' rectangle
- 2: Polka Dot 2½''×4¼'' rectangle
- 3: Dark Blue 2¾''×3¼'' rectangle
- 4: Polka Dot 2''×4¼'' rectangle
- 5: Light Blue 2½'' square

2 Referencing Figure 3 and working in numerical order, paper-piece two of Template C using the following fabrics in each space:

- 1: Dark Blue 2¾''×3½'' rectangle
- 2: Polka Dot 2½''×4¼'' rectangle
- 3: Light Blue 2¾''×3¼'' rectangle
- 4: Polka Dot 2''×4¼'' rectangle
- 5: Dark Blue 2½'' square

3 Repeat Steps 1–2 to create a total of 96 Template B's and 96 Template C's. Employ an organizing system to keep each 4-template unit together.

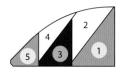

Figure 2.

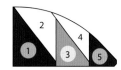

Figure 3.

ASSEMBLING THE SMALL ORANGE PEEL BLOCKS

1 Working with one 4-template unit at a time, sew together a Template B to a Template C along the long, straight edge to make an B/C Unit (Fig. 4). Press seams open.

2 Repeat Step 1 to create a total of 48 B/C units.

3 Referencing Figure 5, sew 2 B/C units together along the remaining straight edge, matching center seams. Press seams open.

4 Pin a Template A Gray Background piece to the completed unit from Step 2, aligning the dots. Sew between the dots, back stitching at each dot (Fig. 6). The short end of the background fabric has been left unsewn intentionally, to aid in piecing the blocks later. Press seams toward the background fabric.

5 Repeat Step 4 on the other side of the block.

6 Trim block to 8½'' square. Use the 45 degree line on your acrylic ruler and the center seam of the block as a guide (Fig. 7).

7 Repeat Steps 1–6 to create a total of 48 Small Orange Peel Blocks.

QUILTER TO QUILTER

For efficiency, paper-piece all 4 units from a set at a time. This will ensure the proper color placement. If paper piecing is new to you, see the instructions on page 10.

Figure 4.

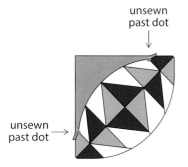

Figure 5.

unsewn
past dot

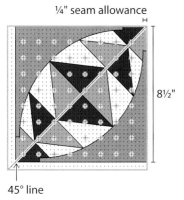

unsewn
past dot

Figure 6.

¼" seam allowance

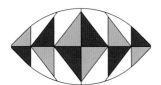

8½"

45° line

Figure 7.

PIECING THE SASHING

1 Referencing Figure 8 and working in numerical order, paper-piece Template D using the following fabrics in each section:

- 1: Polka Dot 3''×3½'' rectangle
- 2 and 3: Gray 2½''×3½'' rectangles
- 4: Assorted Scrap 3''×3½'' rectangle
- 5: Gray 1¾''×5¼'' rectangle
- 6: Gray 1¾''×6½'' rectangle
- 7 and 8: Navy 2½''×3½'' rectangles

2 Trim excess fabric along the seam allowance line and remove papers.

3 Repeat to create a total of 82 sashing strips.

4 Organize the sashing strips together into 18 groups of 4 units each based on the scrap used in Section 4. The remaining 10 sashing strips will contain random scraps in Section 4.

ASSEMBLING QUILT TOP

1 Referencing Figure 11, arrange your pieced units on a design wall or on the floor. Pay very close attention to placing the grouped sashing strips to create the secondary pattern of matching stars. Only the 10 outermost sashing strips will contain the random scraps in Section 4.

2 Sew blocks and sashing into rows. You will use 4 orange peel blocks, 4 matching sashing strips and (1) 2½'' square to create the large orange peel blocks.

3 On each small block, the short end of the Template A background fabric has been left unsewn. This is so you can lightly pull the loose end into the seam allowance as you pin, if necessary. (Fig. 9)

4 Sew rows together to create a large orange peel block. (Fig. 10)

Figure 8.

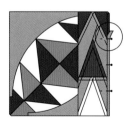

Figure 9.

Figure 10.

5 Repeat to create a total of 12 large orange peel blocks.

6 Sew the large orange peel blocks into 4 rows of 3 blocks each attaching the set aside sashing pairs in-between each block. Press seams open.

7 Sew 6 sashing strips and (5) 2½" squares into 3 rows. Press seams toward squares.

8 Referencing Figure 11, sew block and sashing rows together. Press seams open.

FINISHING

1 Layer the top with backing and batting, baste and quilt as desired.

2 Attach the binding using your favorite method.

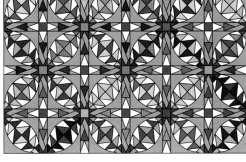

Figure 11.

INSPIRED SCRAPS From Janice Zeller Ryan

I am a sucker for fussy-cutting, so anytime I get to utilize small snippets of my favorite prints, I am happy. My favorite scrap quilt is a Log Cabin House Quilt utilizing a quick and easy tutorial on Sarah's website thehouseofkrom.com. The blocks are perfect for a bee quilt (which was why I chose them), because they are quick, easy, and the bee members could have fun and express themselves in their blocks. I love that my family and I still find little hidden gems in each block.

Made with
SQUARES

ORIGAMI GARDEN

By John Adams

Unlike other quilts I've made, this one did not start with a pattern or fabric selection in mind. This quilt began with the color palette alone and I built the rest from there. With the palette established, I began pulling fabric scraps and fat quarters from my stash (and, admittedly, from a few local quilt shops). The subtle, low-volume background fabric helped to pull the seemingly disparate prints and colors together. I designed a fairly simple block inspired by an origami folded paper flower and constructed simply from half-square triangles and flying geese. When sewing the blocks together I tried to keep the fabric choices as random as possible. Rather than a repeating block pattern, I chose to scatter the flower blocks across the quilt top to resemble a garden. With different color combinations, fabric selections, and variations in block placement, it's easy to make this versatile quilt pattern in your own signature style.

Finished Block Size: 6½'' square

Finished Quilt Size: 66''×78''

MATERIALS

Scraps: Assortment of scraps in a predetermined color palette to yield the required cuts per the Cutting instructions. If using yardage, then 12–14 fat quarters will suffice.

Background fabric: 4 yards

Backing fabric: 5 yards

Binding fabric: ⅔ yard

QUILTER TO QUILTER

You may want to wait until quilt top assembly to cut the 6½'' background squares, as your layout may allow you to cut larger squares and rectangles to comprise the background for more efficient cutting and fabric usage. More in the 'Assembling the Quilt Top' section.

CUTTING

Note: Width of Fabric = WOF

From Assorted Scraps, cut:
- (24) 5½'' squares
- (48) 5'' squares
- (96) 2½''×4½'' rectangles

From Background Fabric, cut:
- (3) 5½''×WOF strips
  - Subcut into (24) 5½'' squares
- (28) 2½''×WOF strips
  - Subcut into (192) 2½'' squares
  - Subcut (96) 2½''×6½'' rectangles
- (8) 6½''×WOF strips
  - Subcut into (47) 6½'' squares

From Binding Fabric, cut:
(8) 2½'' strips

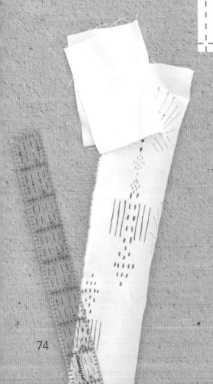

INSPIRED SCRAPS   From John Adams

In my opinion, nobody in the game is working a scrap bin better than Jen Kingwell right now. Her discerning eye when selecting prints and her deft use of color, pattern, and texture make a seemingly random assortment of fabrics sing. All this and the woman knows how to rock a low volume background too. Look around Pinterest for all of the Gypsy Wife, My Small World, and Steampunk quilts that Jen's fans have created in their own scrappy styles. (My friend Megan McNeilly's version of Steampunk comes immediately to mind.) The true magic of Jen's patterns is that everyone's versions always turn out as beautifully as Jen's own.

ASSEMBING THE BLOCK UNITS

The Tulip Block Units

1 Gather (48) 5½'' squares of background fabrics and (48) 5½'' squares of print fabrics. Refer to page 9 to create 48 half-square triangles (or HSTs).

2 Draw a faint diagonal pencil line on the wrong side of the HST units, perpendicular to the seam. (Fig. 1)

3 Pair an HST unit with a 5'' square of a printed fabric. With right sides together, sew a line ¼'' from each side of the drawn line. (Fig. 2)

4 Cut the block in half diagonally along the drawn line. Press your two units open. (Fig. 3)

5 Trim each tulip block down to 4½'' square.

6 Repeat Steps 1–5 for a total of 96 Tulip Blocks.

Figure 1.   Figure 2.

Figure 3.

The Flying Geese Units

1 Referring to page 9 for the flying geese assembly, sew 96 flying geese units using your 2½'' background squares and 2½''×4½'' scrap units. (Fig. 4)

Figure 4.

ASSEMBLING THE BLOCK

1 Referencing Figure 5, join the Tulip Blocks to the flying geese units along the 4½″ edges. Repeat to create a total of 96 units.

2 Sew a 2½″×6½″ background rectangle to the right side of the unit from Step 1 along the 6½″ edge. This is your A Block. Repeat to create a total of 48 A Blocks.

3 Sew a 2½″×6½″ background rectangle to the left side of the unit from Step 1 along the 6½″ edge. This is your B Block. Repeat to make 48 B Blocks.

4 Trim the A and B Blocks to 6½″ square as needed.

ASSEMBLING THE QUILT

1 The quilt top is a grid of 6½″ blocks. You are free to 'plant your own garden' by arranging the pieced and background squares however you like or refer to the Figure 6. Sew the blocks together into 13 rows of 11 blocks each. Sew the rows together, pressing the seams in alternating directions for each row.

FINISHING

1 Layer the top with backing and batting, baste and quilt as desired.

2 Attach the binding using your favorite method.

Figure 5.

A Block: Make 48

B Block: Make 48

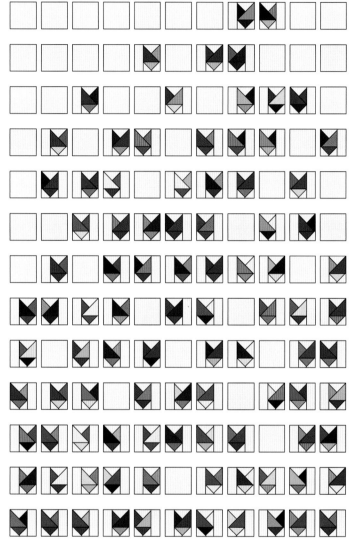

Figure 6.

QUILTER TO QUILTER

If you chose to wait to cut the 6½'' background squares, arrange the pieced blocks into a grid. You will see that the placement of your background squares may allow you to create larger units of background fabric cuts. This can help streamline the cutting and piecing time and maximize your usable yardage.

YOU+ME+US

By Kari Vojtechovsky

Quilted by Christine Perrigo

My favorite reason to make a quilt is as a gift for someone I care about. To me, this design symbolizes the love and life two people share. The quilt features two separate colors but they weave in and out in tandem. This is a lot like two people becoming a family, separate but creating a beautiful life together. This pattern is not only a great way to use any lingering scrap strips, but it can also become a heartfelt gift celebrating a wedding, a birth or an anniversary. Even if you make this quilt for no other reason than liking the dramatic graphic impact it creates, the simple piecing will make this a joy to sew.

Finished Block Size: 42″×43¾″

Finished Quilt Size: 91½″×89¾″

MATERIALS

Assorted Print Scraps: Approximately 2½–3 yards total of various lengths of 2¼" strips (includes binding)

Rust Solid Fabric: 1 yard

Mustard Solid Fabric: 1 yard

Chambray Fabric: 4¼ yards

Backing Fabric: 8¼ yards
(or 3 yards of 108" wide backing)

Batting: 98"×100"

CUTTING

Note: Width of Fabric = WOF

From Assorted Scraps, cut lengths as follows:
- (4) 2¼"×42½" strips (Row Y)
- (4) 2¼"×39" strips
- (4) 2¼"×35½" strips
- (4) 2¼"×32" strips
- (4) 2¼"×28½" strips
- (4) 2¼"×25" strips
- (4) 2¼"×21½" strips
- (4) 2¼"×18" strips
- (4) 2¼"×14½" strips
- (4) 2¼"×11" strips
- (4) 2¼"×7½" strips
- (4) 2¼"×4" strips
- (10) 2¼"×WOF strips or equivalent for binding (must be longer than 370" when sewn together)

INSPIRED SCRAPS   From Kari Vojtechovsky

I love using my scraps to make something small and push myself: a new color combination, a new technique or improving my skills. One new technique I suprised myself with enjoying is the hand appliqué in Aerial Grove by Carolyn Friedlander, found in her *Savor Each Stitch* book. I was able to use small scraps for my circles, including some precious hand screen printed ones from Karen Lewis. The background will make a dent in my low volume scrap pile and small pieces of yardage.

From the Rust and Mustard solid Fabrics, cut (from EACH color):

- (14) 2¼''×WOF strips:
  Subcut into the following lengths:
  - (2) 2¼''×42½'' strips (Row B)
  - (2) 2¼''×39'' strips
  - 2 strips into (2) 2¼''×35½'' strips and (2) 2¼''×4'' strips*
  - 2 strips into (2) 2¼''×32'' strips and (2) 2¼''×7½'' strips*
  - 2 strips into (2) 2¼''×28½'' strips and (2) 2¼''×11'' strips*
  - 2 strips into (2) 2¼''×25'' strips and (2) 2¼''×14½'' strips*
  - 2 strips into (2) 2¼''×21½'' strips and (2) 2¼''×18'' strips*

*One of each size per strip

From Chambray Fabric, cut:

- (5) 4''×WOF strips
  - Subcut one strip in half
- (54) 2¼''×WOF strips:
  Subcut into the following lengths:
  - (6) 2¼''×42½'' rectangles (Row A and sashing)
  - 8 strips into (16) 2¼''×19¾'' strips
  - 8 strips into (16) 2¼''×18'' and (16) 2¼''×2¼'' squares**
  - 8 strips into (16) 2¼''×16¼'' strips and (16) 2¼''×4'' strips**
  - 8 strips into (16) 2¼''×14½'' strips and (16) 2¼''×5¾'' strips **
  - 8 strips into (16) 2¼''×12¾'' strips and (16) 2¼''×7½'' strips**
  - 8 strips into (16) 2¼''×11'' strips and (16) 2¼''×9¼'' strips **

**Two of each size per strip

QUILTER TO QUILTER

Do you have a 2¼'' scrap strip you really want to use but is not long enough for one of the rows? No problem! Sew what you have to another scrap to create the length needed. Leftover scrap strips can be used for the scrappy binding too.

ASSEMBLING THE BLOCKS

1 Sew (2) 2¼''×19¾'' chambray strips to opposite sides of (1) 2¼''×4'' scrap strip, short sides together. Press. This is Row C. (Fig. 1)

Figure 1.

2 Sew (2) 2¼''×2¼'' chambray squares to opposite sides of (1) 2¼''×39'' rust strip, short sides together. Press. This is Row D.

3 Sew (2) 2¼''×18'' chambray strips to opposite sides of (1) 2¼''×7½'' scrap strip, short sides together. Press. This is Row E.

4 Sew (2) 2¼''×4'' chambray strips to opposite sides of (1) 2¼''×35½'' rust strip, short sides together. Press. This is Row F.

5 Sew (2) 2¼''×16¼'' chambray strips to opposite sides of (1) 2¼''×11'' scrap strip, short sides together. Press. This is Row G.

6 Sew (2) 2¼''×5¾'' chambray strips to opposite sides of (1) 2¼''×32'' rust strip, short sides together. Press. This is Row H.

7 Sew (2) 2¼''×14½'' chambray strips to opposite sides of (1) 2¼''×14½'' scrap strip, short sides together. Press. This is Row I.

8 Sew (2) 2¼''×7½'' chambray strips to opposite sides of (1) 2¼''×28½'' rust strip, short sides together. Press. This is Row J.

9 Sew (2) 2¼''×12¾'' chambray strips to opposite sides of (1) 2¼''×18'' scrap strip, short sides together. Press. This is Row K.

10 Sew (2) 2¼''×9¼'' chambray strips to opposite sides of (1) 2¼''×25'' rust strip, short sides together. Press. This is Row L.

11 Sew (2) 2¼''×11'' chambray strips to opposite sides of (1) 2¼''×21½'' scrap strip, short sides together. Press. This is Row M.

12 Sew (2) 2¼''×11'' chambray strips to opposite sides of (1) 2¼''×21½'' rust strip, short sides together. Press. This is Row N.

13 Sew (2) 2¼''×9¼'' chambray strips to opposite sides of (1) 2¼''×25'' scrap strip, short sides together. Press. This is Row O.

14 Sew (2) 2¼''×12¾'' chambray strips to opposite sides of (1) 2¼''×18'' rust strip, short sides together. Press. This is Row P.

15 Sew (2) 2¼''×7½'' chambray strips to opposite sides of (1) 2¼''×28½'' scrap strip, short sides together. Press. This is Row Q.

Row Assembly Cheat Sheet

	Chambray	Rust	Scrap	Chambray	Assembly Visual
A	2¼"×42½"				
B		2¼"×42½"			
C	2¼"×19¾"		2¼"×4"	2¼"×19¾"	
D	2¼"×2¼"	2¼"×39"		2¼"×2¼"	
E	2¼"×18"		2¼"×7½"	2¼"×18"	
F	2¼"×4"	2¼"×35½"		2¼"×4"	
G	2¼"×16¼"		2¼"×11"	2¼"×16¼"	
H	2¼"×5¾"	2¼"×32"		2¼"×5¾"	
I	2¼"×14½"		2¼"×14½"	2¼"×14½"	
J	2¼"×7½"	2¼"×28½"		2¼"×7½"	
K	2¼"×12¾"		2¼"×18"	2¼"×12¾"	
L	2¼"×9¼"	2¼"×25"		2¼"×9¼"	
M	2¼"×11"		2¼"×21½"	2¼"×11"	
N	2¼"×11"	2¼"×21½"		2¼"×11"	
O	2¼"×9¼"		2¼"×25"	2¼"×9¼"	
P	2¼"×12¾"	2¼"×18"		2¼"×12¾"	
Q	2¼"×7½"		2¼"×28½"	2¼"×7½"	
R	2¼"×14½"	2¼"×14½"		2¼"×14½"	
S	2¼"×5¾"		2¼"×32"	2¼"×5¾"	
T	2¼"×16¼"	2¼"×11"		2¼"×16¼"	
U	2¼"×4"		2¼"×35½"	2¼"×4"	
V	2¼"×18"	2¼"×7½"		2¼"×18"	
W	2¼"×2¼"		2¼"×39"	2¼"×2¼"	
X	2¼"×19¾"	2¼"×4"		2¼"×19¾"	
Y			2¼"×42½"		

16 Sew (2) 2¼''×14½'' chambray strips to opposite sides of (1) 2¼''×14½'' rust strip, short sides together. Press. This is Row R.

17 Sew (2) 2¼''×5¾'' chambray strips to opposite sides of (1) 2¼''×32'' scrap strip, short sides together. Press. This is Row S.

18 Sew (2) 2¼''×16¼'' chambray strips to opposite sides of (1) 2¼''×11'' rust strip, short sides together. Press. This is Row T.

19 Sew (2) 2¼''×4'' chambray strips to opposite sides of (1) 2¼''×35½'' scrap strip, short sides together. Press. This is Row U.

20 Sew (2) 2¼''×18'' chambray strips to opposite sides of (1) 2¼''×7½'' rust strip, short sides together. Press. This is Row V.

21 Sew (2) 2¼''chambray squares to opposite sides of (1) 2¼''×39'' scrap strip, short sides together. Press. This is Row W.

22 Sew (2) 2¼''×19¾'' chambray strips to opposite sides of (1) 2¼''×4'' rust strip, short sides together. Press. This is Row X.

23 Referencing Figure 2, sew together Rows A–Y in order. This creates 1 rust block.

24 Repeat Steps 1–23 to make the second rust block.

25 Repeat Steps 1–24 substituting the mustard fabric for the rust fabric to create 2 mustard blocks.

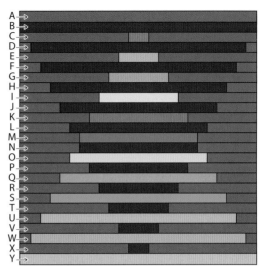

Figure 2.

ASSEMBLING THE QUILT TOP

1 Referring to Figure 3, sew the rust blocks together with (1) 2¼''×42½'' chambray sashing strip between each block. (Note that the bottom block is turned 180°.) Press all seams of rust column down.

2 Repeat Step 1 with the mustard blocks. Press all seams of yellow column up.

3 Sew the rust column to the mustard column, nesting the seams.

4 Trim off the selvedges and sew (2) 4''×WOF strips and (1) 4''× half-length WOF strip on the short ends. Press. Repeat. Trim both to create (2) 4''×89¾'' strips.

5 Sew (1) 4''×89¾'' strip to the left of the rust column and one to the right of the mustard column. Press.

FINISHING

1 Layer the top with backing and batting, baste and quilt as desired.

2 Attach the binding using your favorite method.

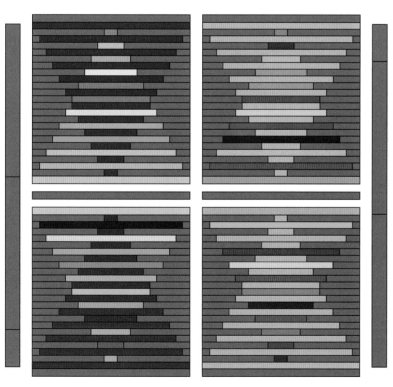

Figure 3.

CONFETTI

By Kati Spencer

I love quilting with triangles and the different design options this shape provides. I've made other projects in the past with equilateral triangles, but always of the same size. With Confetti I wanted to mix it up. This pattern incorporates finished equilateral triangles 2″, 4″ and 6″ in height, plus trapezoids in low volume fabrics which allow the triangles to really pop. These shapes are combined to create 12″ finished triangle "blocks" that are not emphasized in the overall design, but make this improv style triangle quilt manageable even for someone new to triangles.

While I enjoy scrappy quilts and the idea of using all the scraps in my bucket, that is not my overall style. I felt this quilt needed a specific color palette to pull it all together and allow the triangles to stand out against the low volume background. When cleaning out my purse one day, I realized the perfect color combination was all right there in front of me. My purse is navy with tan straps and gold hardware, my wallet is bright pink, my lip balm container is a pale pink, and my water bottle is mint green. Inspiration truly is everywhere!

Finished Quilt Size: 56″×72″

MATERIALS

Background Fabric: 2½ yards or a large variety of low volume scrap strip lengths either 2½'' or 4½'' wide.

Triangle Fabrics: Large selection of scrap fabrics ranging in size from 2½''×3½'' to 6½''×8½'' or at least 25 fat eighths.

Binding Fabric: ½ yard

Backing Fabric: 4½ yards

Batting: 64''×80''

CUTTING

Note: Width of Fabric = WOF

See Template pages 124–125 and Figures 1–3 for placement

From Background Fabric, cut:
- (20) 2½''×WOF strips
  - Subcut 116 trapezoids from (13) 2½'' strips using Template D
  - Subcut 44 trapezoids from (8) 2½'' strips using Template E
- (6) 4½'' strips
  - Subcut into 62 triangles using Template B

From various Scrap Fabrics or Fat Eighths, cut:
- (139) 2½'' triangles using Template A
- (92) 4½'' triangles using Template B
- (37) 6½'' triangles using Template C
- (13) 4½'' half-triangles using Template F and (23) 4½'' half-triangles using Template F in reverse

From Binding Fabric, cut:
- (7) 2½''×WOF strips

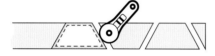

Figure 1: Template D.

Figure 2: Template E.

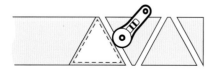

Figure 3: Template B.

Using a 60° Acrylic Triangle Ruler

Although templates are provided for this pattern, a clear acrylic 60° equilateral triangle ruler could save some time. Templates correlate to the ruler as follows:

- Template A: Cut triangles from 2½'' strips, centering between top of ruler and 2½'' line.

- Template B: Cut triangles from 4½'' strips, centering between top of ruler and 4½'' line.

- Template C: Cut triangles from 6½'' strips, centering between top of ruler and 6½'' line.

- Template D: Cut trapezoids from 2½'' strip, centering between 2'' and 4½'' lines.

- Template E: Cut trapezoids from 2½'' strip, centering between 4'' and 6½'' lines.

- Template F: Cut the 90° triangles by arranging fabric on the 4½'' ruler line and the dashed lines right or left of the center line. Trim fabric along the opposite angled line.

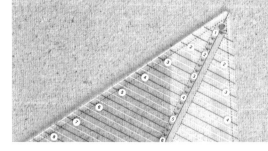

QUILTER TO QUILTER

This quilt has many bias edges. To minimize stretching and distortion and ensure accurate cutting, try lightly starching and ironing the fabric before cutting. Press seams carefully. Do not push the fabric or slide the iron, merely press.

ASSEMBLING THE TRIANGLE BLOCK

1 Working on one block at a time, select fabrics and arrange the pieces as shown in the following diagrams.

2 Sew the shapes into the smaller sections first and then piece the completed sections to finish each block. Press seams open or to side as desired. Pressing open in some cases will reduce bulky seams when multiple points intersect.

Create the following block quantities:
- (12) Block 1
- (7) Block 2
- (11) Block 3
- (12) Block 4
- (1) Block 5
- (5) Block 6
- (5) Block 7
- (1) Block 8

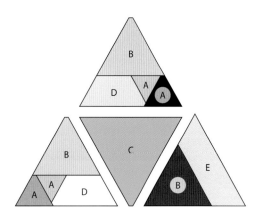

Block 1.

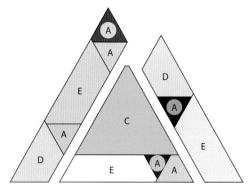

Block 2.

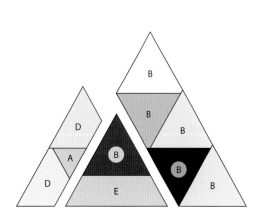

Block 3.

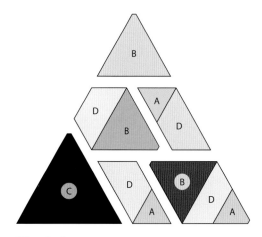

Block 4.

QUILTER TO QUILTER

Triangle Piecing Tips: Piecing triangles can be tricky. To ensure that the finished quilt has sharp, clean points, pin at all of the intersections. When arranging triangles or piecing, pull back the seam allowance before pinning to ensure the points are accurately aligned where they will meet once stitched. Always sew the triangle pieces with the grain running vertically in relation to the block itself.

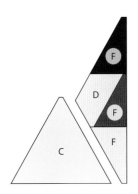

Block 5.

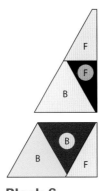

Block 6.

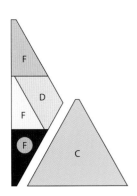

Block 7.

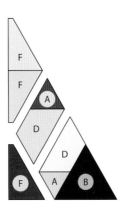

Block 8.

ASSEMBLING THE QUILT TOP

1 Using a design wall or a floor, arrange the blocks as desired or refer to Figure 4 for placement. Rotate the orientation of some blocks to create more variety and arrange the blocks so that all of the colors are fairly evenly spaced throughout the quilt. You may also choose to create a secondary design by adjusting color placement.

2 Sew the first row of pieced triangles together. Pin at all of the intersections, carefully matching the points. Press. Repeat for the remaining five rows. Sew all the rows together, again pinning at all of the intersections. Press seams.

FINISHING

1 Layer the top with backing and batting, baste and quilt as desired.

2 Attach the binding using your favorite method.

INSPIRED SCRAPS From Kati Spencer

One of my favorite scrappy quilts that I ever made was created using a simple Strings Block tutorial I saw first on the Film in the Fridge blog by Ashley Newcomb. This quilt was one of my first quilts, but I was surprised by how quickly the scraps had already piled up from previous projects. It was a great use for both smaller and larger scrap strips. I love looking at this quilt and remembering my early projects that each fabric came from. The block is easy to create and is foundation pieced to ensure straight seams with very minimal distortion and stretching. The great thing about this pattern is the flexibility. Each Strings Quilt looks so different and allows the quilter to add their own flair depending on the colors and fabrics, the strip widths and the setting style selected. Making a new Strings Quilt is on my to-do list for another day.

Figure 4.

QUILTER TO QUILTER
- -
How you arrange your sewn blocks is up to you. You may want to arrange the blocks such that all colors are fairly evenly spaced throughout the quilt, or you may choose to create a secondary design by adjusting color placement. One day I hope to create an ombré version of this quilt. I'd love to progress the colors of the triangles from light to dark in the overall design.

Made with
SQUARES

DIVISION STREET
DIAMONDS

**By Katie
Blakesley**

*Quilted by
Abby Latimer*

This quilt was inspired by my family's short time in Portland, Oregon. We lived just off of Division Street in Southeast Portland, a vibrant, walkable community. The diamond shapes reminded me of both the individuality and the cohesiveness of the neighborhood. If you sat out on your porch for long enough, you were sure to see something interesting. Scrap quilts are a little bit like that— the more you look at them, the more the variation in fabrics, colors, and other subtle differences appear and you can see the personality of the maker coming through to create something unique.

Finished Quilt Size: 67"×78"

MATERIALS

White Solid: 4½ yards

Assorted Aqua Scraps: ½ yard

Assorted Coral Scraps: ¼ yard

Assorted Tan Scraps: ⅛ yard

Assorted Yellow Scraps: ⅛ yard

Backing Fabric: 5½ yards

Binding Fabric: ¾ yard

Batting: 75"×90"

CUTTING

Note: Width of Fabric = WOF

From White Solid, cut:
Cut the long white strips (measuring 78") first.
- (1) 32½"× 78" rectangle
- (1) 7½"×78" rectangle
- (19) 3"×WOF strips;
  Subcut into:
  - (8) 3"×13" rectangles [A]
  - (12) 3"×10½" rectangles [B]
  - (12) 3"×8" rectangles [C]
  - (12) 3"×5½" rectangles [D]
  - (87) 3"×3" squares [E]

From Aqua Scraps, cut:
- (5) 3"×WOF strips
  - Subcut (58) 3"×3" squares [F]

From Coral Scraps, cut:
- (2) 3"×WOF strips
  - Subcut (24) 3"×3" squares [G]

From Tan Scraps, cut:
- (1) 3"×WOF strip
  - Subcut (12) 3"×3" squares [H]

From Yellow Scraps cut:
- (1) 3"×WOF strip
  - Subcut (12) 3"×3" squares [I]

From Binding Fabric, cut:
(8) 2½"×WOF strips

QUILTER TO QUILTER

Fabric selection: This design works best using solids, tone on tone prints, or color plus white prints. Using large prints or busy individual prints makes the overall diamond design harder to see. Arrange the three diamonds on a design wall or floor and play with the fabric placement making sure you have a good balance and contrast.

ASSEMBLING THE ROWS

Using Figure 1 for color and unit placement, sew pieces along the short sides in the following order. Press seams toward the darker fabric.

1 Sew 4 of Row 1 in this order: A, F, A. Press.

2 Sew 6 of Row 2 in this order: B, F, E, F, B. Press.

3 Sew 4 of Row 3 in this order: C, F, E, G, E, F, C. Press.

4 Sew 4 of Row 4 in this order: D, F, E, G, E, G, E, F, D. Press.

5 Sew 4 of Row 5 in this order: E, F, E, G, E, I, E, G, E, F, E. Press.

6 Sew 2 of Row 6 in this order: F, E, G, E, I, E, I, E, G, E, F. Press.

7 Sew 2 of Row 7 in this order: C, F, E, H, E, F, C. Press.

8 Sew 2 of Row 8 in this order: D, F, E, H, E, H, E, F, D. Press.

9 Sew 2 of Row 9 in this order: E, F, E, H, E, I, E, H, E, F, E. Press.

10 Sew 1 of Row 10 together in this order: F, E, H, E, I, E, I, E, H, E, F. Press.

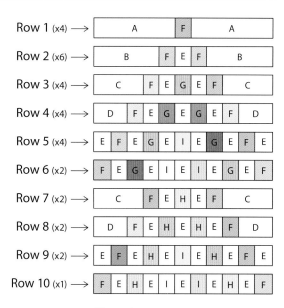

Figure 1.

ASSEMBLING THE DIAMONDS

1 To assemble Diamond 1, sew together 11 rows in this order: 1, 2, 3, 4, 5, 6, 5, 4, 3, 2, 1, as shown in Figure 2. Press all row seams the same direction.

2 Repeat Step 1 to assemble Diamond 3.

3 To assemble Diamond 2, sew together 9 rows in this order: 2, 7, 8, 9, 10, 9, 8, 7, and 2, as shown in Figure 3. Press all row seams in the same direction.

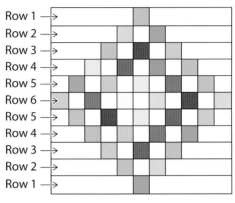

Row 1 →
Row 2 →
Row 3 →
Row 4 →
Row 5 →
Row 6 →
Row 5 →
Row 4 →
Row 3 →
Row 2 →
Row 1 →

Figure 2.

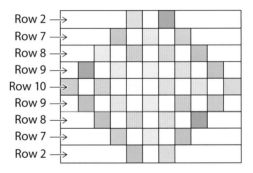

Row 2 →
Row 7 →
Row 8 →
Row 9 →
Row 10 →
Row 9 →
Row 8 →
Row 7 →
Row 2 →

Figure 3.

ASSEMBLING THE QUILT TOP

1 Sew Diamond 1 to Diamond 2, pinning in seams as needed. Press.

2 Sew Diamond 3 to Diamond 2, pinning in seams as needed. Press.

3 Sew the 32½"×78" white solid rectangle to the left of the diamond stack, pinning as needed. Press.

5 Sew the 7½"×78" white solid rectangle to the right side of the diamond stack, pinning as needed. Press. (Fig. 4)

FINISHING

1 Layer the top with backing and batting, baste and quilt as desired.

2 Attach the binding using your favorite method.

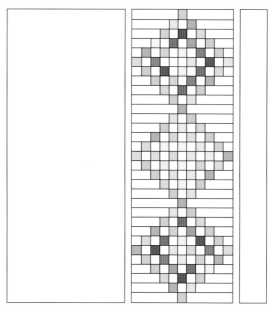

Figure 4.

INSPIRED SCRAPS From Katie Blakesley

I love making small projects using up my scraps (zipper pouches are my favorite quick scrap project). But every once in a while, I want to do something more, and create something a little more permanent. I love scrap quilts because they are so easy to personalize—change up the color scheme or the size of the pieces in any pattern you want to make a scrappy version of and you have a treasured quilt that you can call your own!

Made with
STRIPS

NORTHERN MIGRATION

By Melissa Lunden

This fun twist on the classic flying geese block is perfect for using up some of your smallest scraps. The idea of small triangles for a quilt top has been brewing in my head for a while. Using scraps for this design is a fabulous way to make this quilt and use up some of my favorite fabrics from my scrap basket.

The arrow blocks are easy to sew once you get the hang of them. Try a practice block or two to feel comfortable if this is your first time working with angles. The pattern can be easily modified to be bigger or smaller, depending on your project.

I went through my scrap collection and looked for my favorite color palate of aqua, turquoise, coral, green, blue, magenta and added a little gold to make it fancy. This design really thrives with a nice, high contrast between the scrap arrows and the background color. Grab your favorite colors and have fun with your color story.

Finished Block Size: 7"×4½"

Finished Quilt Size: 63½"×77"

MATERIALS

Assorted Scraps: 1¼ yards made up of at least 11 coordinating prints

Background Fabric: 3½ yards

Binding Fabric: ⅝ yard

Backing Fabric: 4½ yards

Batting: 71''×85''

CUTTING

Note: Width of Fabric = WOF

From Scraps, cut:
- (154) 6''×1½'' rectangles—6 pairs for 9 of the prints and 7 pairs for 2 of the prints. Be sure to keep these groupings organized into matching pairs.

From Background Fabric, cut:
- (4) 3½''×WOF strips for Triangle A
  - Subcut (39) 3½'' squares, then cut the squares in half on the diagonal for a total of 77 small triangles
- (10) 5''×WOF strips Triangle B
  - Subcut (77) 5'' squares, then cut the squares in half on the diagonal for a total of 144 large triangles
- (16) 1½''×WOF strips for the top of the arrow block
  - Subcut (77) 7½''×1½'' rectangles
- (16) 5''×WOF strips for the large solid rectangles
  - Subcut (76) 7½''×5'' rectangles

Cutting Binding:
- Cut (8) 2½''×WOF strips

QUILTER TO QUILTER

Each arrow block is made up of a pair of scraps. I made each block with two pieces from the same print, but you could just as easily make each arrow block with two different prints. It would really make the quilt look even more scrappy and charming.

MAKING THE ARROW BLOCKS

1 Sew one scrap piece to one side of Triangle A. Press seams open.

2 Sew the second scrap piece to the second side of Triangle A. Press seams open.

3 Trim the bottom off the scrap pieces along the bottom line of Triangle A. (Fig. 1)

4 Center and sew the long side of Triangle B to one of the scrap pieces. Press seams open. (Fig. 2)

5 Center and sew a second Triangle B to the other side of the unit. (Fig. 3)

6 Square up your block so it measures 7½"×4". (Fig. 4)

7 Sew the 7½"×1½" rectangle to the top of the block. Press the seams open. (Fig. 5)

8 Square up your blocks, if necessary, so they measure 7½"×5".

9 Repeat Steps 1–8 to create a total of 77 Arrow Blocks.

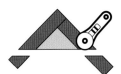

Figure 1.

Figure 2.

Figure 3.

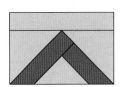

Figure 4.

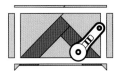

Figure 5.

QUILTER TO QUILTER

For a quick and easy way to make sure your two pieces are lined up in the center, try this trick. Taking care not to stretch the bias edges, fold the sides of the triangles you are sewing in half and finger press at the center. Match up the pinches for perfect centering every time.

QUILTER TO QUILTER

If your scraps have directional prints, be sure to sew them all in the same orientation. That way, you don't find yourself with upside down animals or something else a little distracting.

ASSEMBLING THE QUILT TOP

1 Referencing Figure 6, arrange your Arrow Blocks and rectangles on a design wall or the floor. Alternate beginning each column with an arrow block and a solid rectangle.

2 Once you are happy with your arrangement, sew each of the rows together. Press the seams open.

3 Sew your rows together two at a time. Pin the rows at the seams between the blocks to make sure your rows align perfectly. Press the seams open.

4 Continue to sew all of the rows together until your quilt top is finished.

QUILTING SUGGESTIONS

For this quilt, I used my favorite, tight, wide, zigzag quilting pattern for the entire quilt. I wanted to keep the angles of the triangles and give the solid grey fabric a little texture at the same time. Other fun quilting ideas would be to outline the arrows with larger triangles or create some really clean lines with matchstick echo quilting.

FINISHING

1 Layer the top with backing and batting, baste and quilt as desired.

2 Attach the binding using your favorite method.

3 Love and share your gorgeous new quilt!

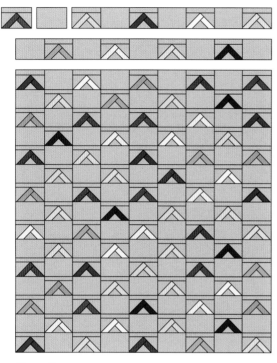

Figure 6.

Quilt Layout: 153 blocks comprised of 77 arrow blocks and 76 rectangles arranged in 17 rows of 9 block each.

QUILTER TO QUILTER

I went for an overall balance of colors with all of my arrows pointing in the same direction. There are so many other fun ways to arrange the Arrow Blocks. Creating a rainbow design or an ombré effect with your colors would be stunning. Playing around with the direction of the arrows would also make for some really interesting designs. Alternate the directions of the arrows of an entire column or row, or just rotate one or two for a little whimsical fun.

INSPIRED SCRAPS From Melissa Lunden

I was massively influenced by Denyse Schmidt and her book, *Quilts*. I still remember standing in my apartment and seeing it for the first time. My sewing brain just sort of exploded. Up until then, I loved to sew clothes and bags, but when I saw what she was doing with patchwork, my heart skipped a beat and I was pretty much hooked from the moment I flipped through her book. Denyse is able to make scrap-filled projects that look timeless, yet fresh at the same time. I love quilts that feature gorgeous designer collections, but there is something so true to the origin of quilting when a project is made using leftover scraps. It is all about the merging of design, function and maximizing resources by reusing fabrics. Denyse continues to offer many inspirational patterns and ideas perfectly suited to use all of my scraps.

Made with
STRIPS

BLACKLIGHT

By Nydia Kehnle

Quilted by Gina Pina

I have a special affection for all things neon and bright. They tend to bring me back to my childhood. Memories of running through the fun house while streaks of lights bounce from mirror to mirror is what inspired the design and color scheme. I selected black and white prints to make the colors pop. I was inspired to create a design that was helpful in scrap busting both larger pieces of fabric and also thin strips. In my studio, the fabrics that I have the hardest time storing are those that are smaller than a fat quarter but larger than anything I want to throw into my small scrap storage bin. This is the perfect project for those thin strips and uses those larger scraps for the background.

Finished Block Size: 9"x 7"

Finished Quilt Size: 54"x 70"

MATERIALS

Scrap Fabrics: see chart at right

Binding Fabric: ½ yard

Backing Fabric: 4 yards

Batting: 62"×78"

Copy paper

QUILTER TO QUILTER

Using color and contrast in different ways can give your quilt a variety of results. Consider using your busy multicolored prints with solid white throughout the entire quilt… or a more planned placement in which you use specific colors in specific template sections to create secondary designs.

CUTTING

Note: Width of Fabric = WOF

From Scraps cut 60 each:

Template Section	Size	Fabric
1	4½"×9"	background
2	1¼"x10"	color strip
3	4"x12½"	background
4	1¼"x12¼"	color strip
5	5"x12¼"	background
6	1¼"×7"	color strip
7	3"x 7"	background

From Binding Fabric, cut:
• (7) 2½"×WOF strips

PREPARATION

See page 126–127 for templates. Print 30 copies of Template A and 30 copies of Template B on copy paper or paper specifically made for paper foundation piecing.

QUILTER TO QUILTER

When paper piecing, I use a 90/14 size needle and a stitch length of 1.6–1.8mm to help make the paper removal easier.

ASSEMBLING THE BLOCK

1 Using Template A (see page 126) and Template B (see page 127), follow the paper piecing instructions on page 10 to piece your blocks.

2 Trim your block around the seam allowance.

3 Create 30 of each block.

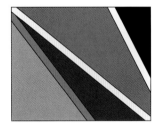

A Block: Make 30.

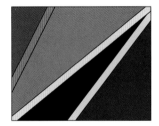

B Block: Make 30.

QUILTER TO QUILTER

I like removing the paper from the back of the blocks once the entire quilt top is pieced because I think it adds some much needed stability. If you prefer to remove the paper once the blocks are trimmed, there are fewer seams to deal with, but your blocks are more prone to shift, so handle them carefully.

ASSEMBLING THE QUILT TOP

1 Referring to Figure 1, sew the blocks together into 10 rows of 6 blocks each. Half of the rows will begin with Template A and half will begin with Template B.

2 Press seams in alternating directions for each row.

3 Sew the rows together, nesting seams. Press seams open.

FINISHING

1 Remove the paper from the back of the quilt top.

2 Layer the top with backing and batting, baste and quilt as desired.

2 Attach the binding using your favorite method.

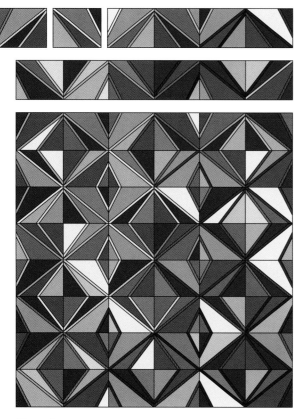

Figure 1.

Modern Hexies, the design created by Nicole Daksiewicz, is one of my favorite projects to make using my smallest scraps. I think her technique is innovative and yet easy to apply to any size of sewing project—zipper pouches, pillows, artwork... the ideas are endless. I think this a great way to use up your favorite random scraps and still keep a modern aesthetic. Nicole has an online tutorial for this innovative applique method on her website: modernhandcraft.com

CALIFORNIA DREAMIN'

By Sherri McConnell

Quilted by Marion Bott

Scrap quilts are my favorites—there is nothing like a scrappy quilt pattern that gives you several options for using those scraps. The basis for this scrap quilt is a bordered 4-Patch unit along with several flying geese units. Also, the placement of the light fabrics creates stars throughout the quilt. There are lots of options with this quilt: make and collect 4-Patch units in a variety of colors, then group similar 4-Patch units with contrasting colored flying geese sections. Or, make all of the 4-Patch units for the whole quilt in a similar colorway creating a chain effect through the quilt. You can also use two different colors along with a background for each block giving another fun, scrappy look. The possibilities are endless, and since the blocks are pieced with the majority of fabrics at 2½'' wide, this quilt is perfect for using up extra jelly roll strips, charm squares, and layer cake squares.

Finished Block Size: 16'' square

Finished Quilt Size: 80½''× 80½'''

MATERIALS

Fabric A: Light Background solid: 5¾ yards (this can also be made up of a combination of fabrics]

Fabric B: Print fabric scraps: 1¾ yards

Fabric C: Print fabric scraps: 2⅔ yards

Binding Fabric: ¾ yard (or at least 336″ prepared binding)

Backing Fabric: 7½ yards

Batting: 88″×88″

CUTTING

Note: Width of Fabric = WOF

From Fabric A, cut:
- (22) 4½″×WOF strips
  - Subcut 3 into (25) 4½″ squares for Block Centers
  - Subcut 19 into (300) 2½″×4½″ rectangles (200 for 4-Patch units and 100 for the Reverse Flying Geese units)
- (25) 2½″×WOF strips
  - Subcut into (400) 2½″ squares (200 for the 4-Patch units and 200 for the Flying Geese units)

From Fabric B, cut:
- (300) 2½″ squares for the 4-Patch units

From Fabric C, cut:
- (200) 2½″×4½″ rectangles for the Flying Geese units
- (200) 2½″ squares for the Reverse Flying Geese units

From Binding, cut:
- (9) 2½″×WOF strips

ASSEMBLING THE FOUR-PATCH UNITS

1 Using (2) 2½'' background squares and (2) 2½'' print squares, sew a 4-Patch unit. (Fig. 1)

2 Attach a 2½''×4½'' Fabric A rectangle to the left side of the 4-Patch unit. (Fig. 2)

3 Repeat Steps 1–2 to create a total of 100 units.

4 Sew the remaining (100) 2½''×4½'' background rectangles to the remaining 2½'' print squares.

5 Sew the 100 units from Step 4 to the 100 4-Patch units from Step 3. Each unit should measure 6½''×6½''. Repeat to create a total of 100 bordered 4-Patch units. (Fig. 3)

ASSEMBLING THE FLYING GEESE UNITS

1 See page 9 for instructions on assembling the Flying Geese Units.

2 Using (2) 2½'' background squares and (1) 2½''×4½'' print rectangle, follow instructions for constructing flying geese. Repeat to make (100) 2½''×4½'' flying geese units.

3 Sew the reverse flying geese units by using (2) 2½'' print squares and (1) 2½''×4½'' background rectangle. Repeat to make (100) 2½''×4½'' reverse flying geese units.

4 Sew together 1 flying geese unit, (1) 2½''×4½'' Fabric A rectangle, and 1 reverse flying geese unit to make one block section. Sections will measure 4½''×6½''. Repeat to make a total of 100 block sections. (Fig. 4)

Figure 1.

Figure 2.

Figure 3.

Flying Geese: Make 100

Reverse Flying Geese: Make 100

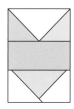

Figure 4.

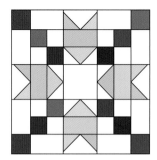

Figure 5.

ASSEMBLING THE QUILT BLOCK

1 Referencing Figure 5 and using 4 bordered 4-Patch units, 4 Flying Geese and Reverse Flying Geese sections and the 4½'' Fabric A squares, assemble the quilt block. Repeat to create a total of 25 blocks.

ASSEMBLING THE QUILT TOP

1 Arrange the 25 blocks into 5 rows of 5 blocks each. At this time you can rearrange for color placement.

2 Sew the blocks together in rows. Press the seams open.

3 Sew the rows together. Press the seams open. (Fig. 6)

4 Since this quilt does not have borders, it helps to stay-stitch ⅛'' all around the edges of the quilt top. This will ensure the top doesn't shift before and during quilting.

FINISHING

1 Layer the top with backing and batting, baste and quilt as desired.

2 Attach the binding using your favorite method.

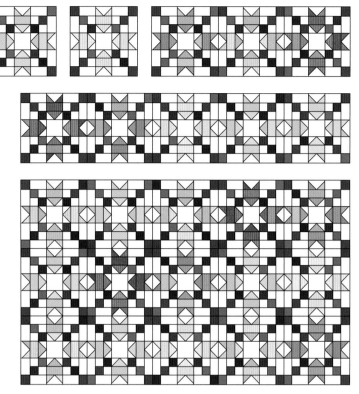

Figure 6.

INSPIRED SCRAPS From Sherri McConnell

It's no secret that I love scraps. The more you use them, the more you seem to have! I usually organize my scraps in bins based on their size. When I use them I enjoy creating small patchwork bags and often piece a patchwork section from scraps for the body of the bag. I also love to make placemats and pillows which are easily made from scraps. But my all-time favorite way to use my leftover scraps (especially those smaller ones) is to make paper pieced hexagons (or hexies). They are quick to sew and if you make a bunch after each larger project, you will soon have a big collection that you can use to create Grandmother's Flower Garden blocks or Dresden plates.

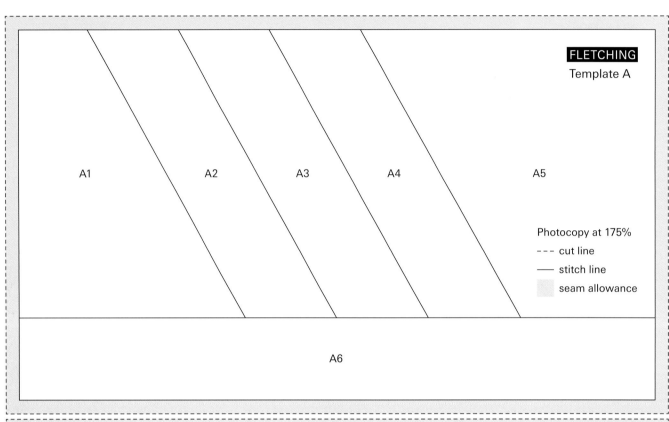

FLETCHING
Template A

A1 A2 A3 A4 A5

Photocopy at 175%
--- cut line
— stitch line
■ seam allowance

A6

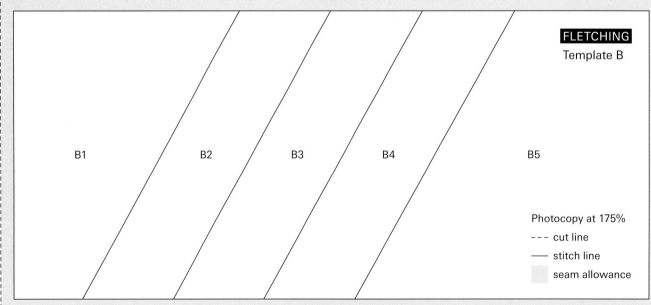

FLETCHING
Template B

B1 B2 B3 B4 B5

Photocopy at 175%
--- cut line
— stitch line
■ seam allowance

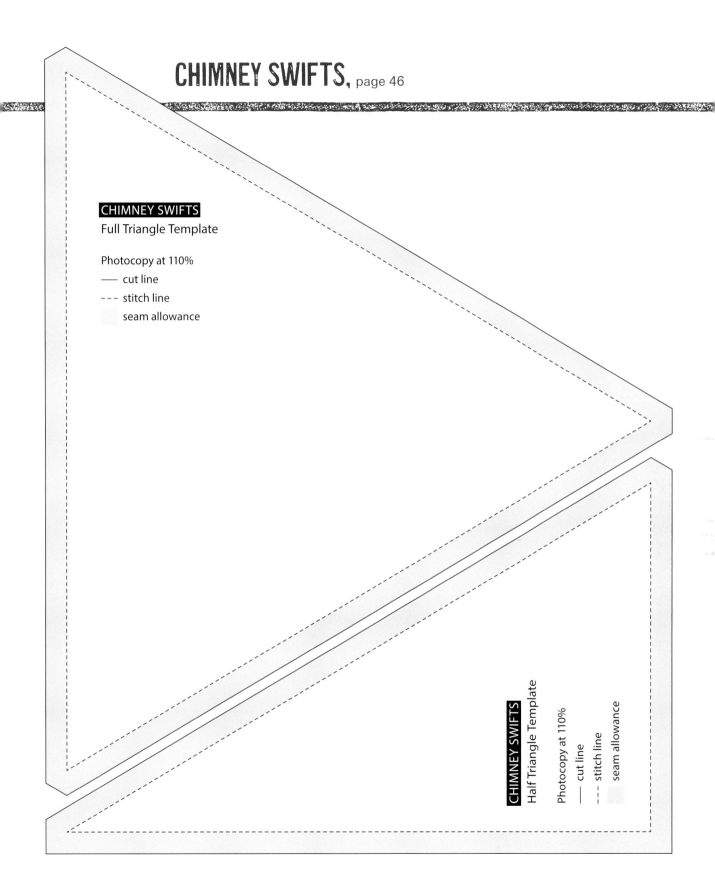

CHIMNEY SWIFTS

Full Triangle Template

Photocopy at 110%
—— cut line
--- stitch line
      seam allowance

CHIMNEY SWIFTS

Half Triangle Template

Photocopy at 110%
—— cut line
--- stitch line
      seam allowance

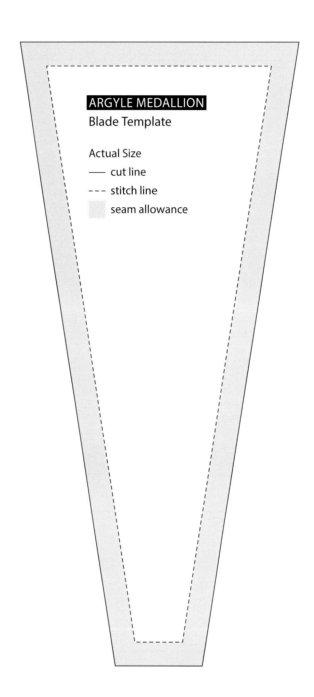

ARGYLE MEDALLION
Blade Template

Actual Size
—— cut line
--- stitch line
[ ] seam allowance

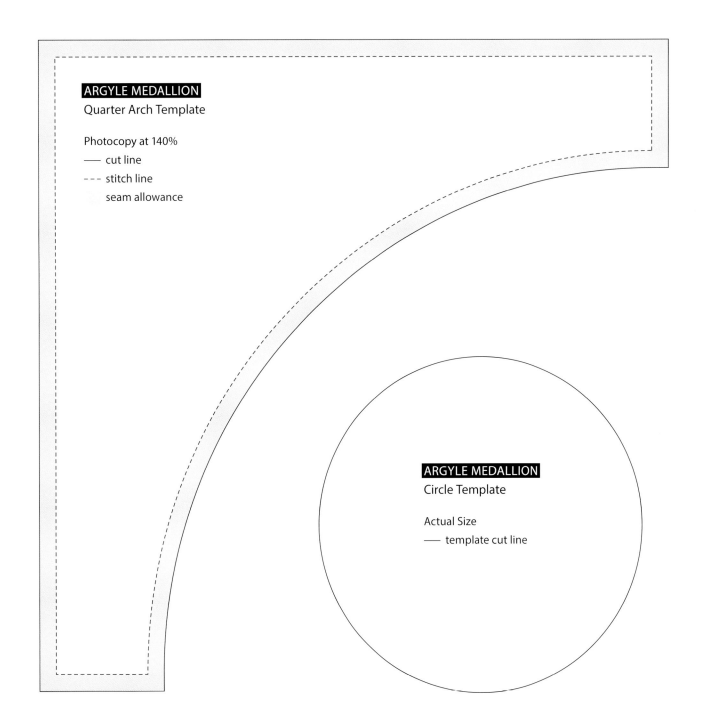

ARGYLE MEDALLION
Quarter Arch Template

Photocopy at 140%
—— cut line
--- stitch line
    seam allowance

ARGYLE MEDALLION
Circle Template

Actual Size
—— template cut line

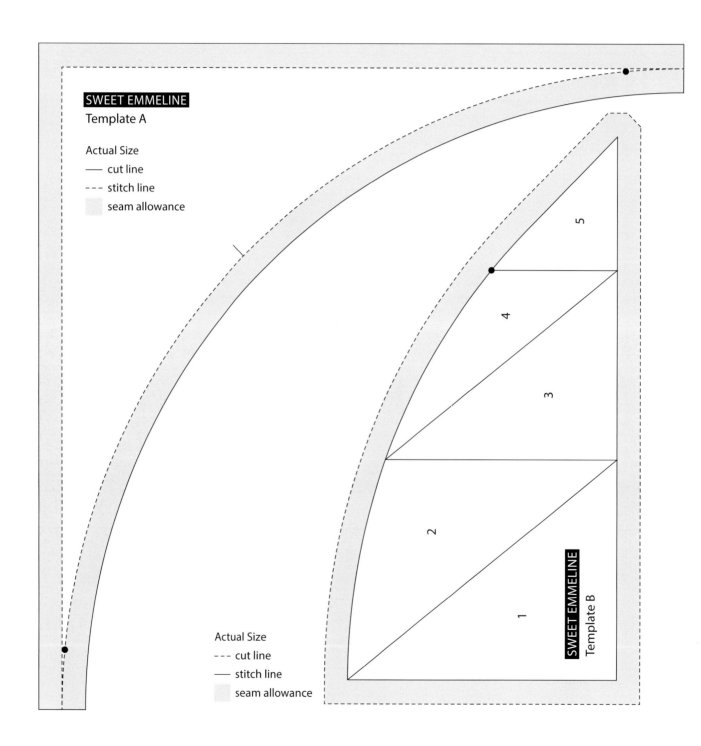

SWEET EMMELINE
Template A

Actual Size
— cut line
- - - stitch line
seam allowance

5

4

3

2

1

SWEET EMMELINE
Template B

Actual Size
- - - cut line
— stitch line
seam allowance

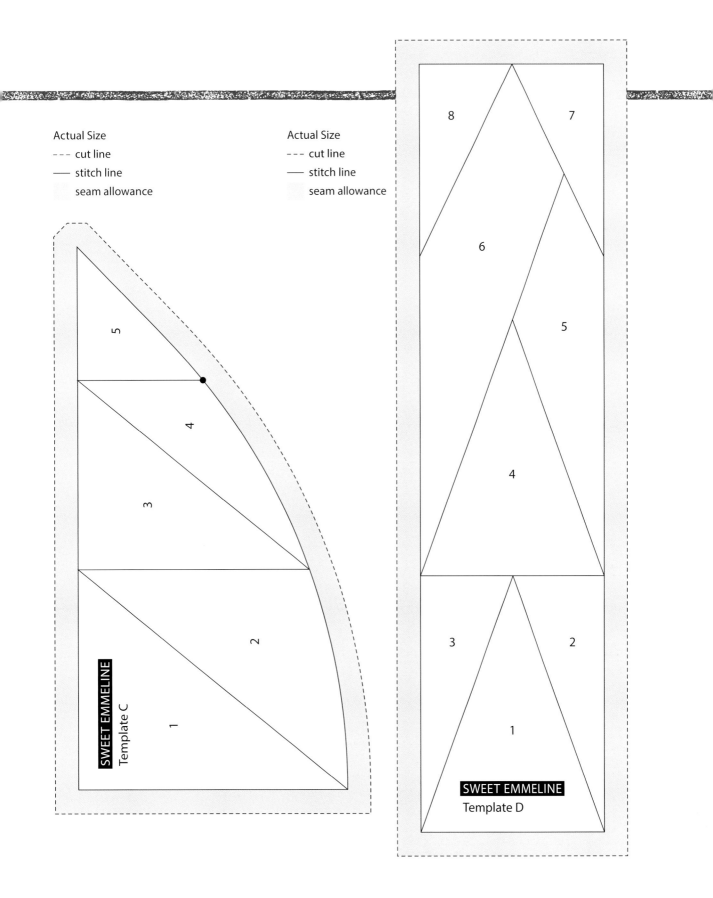

Actual Size
- - - cut line
—— stitch line
seam allowance

Actual Size
- - - cut line
—— stitch line
seam allowance

SWEET EMMELINE
Template C

5

4

3

2

1

8   7

6

5

4

3   2

1

SWEET EMMELINE
Template D

CONFETTI, page 86

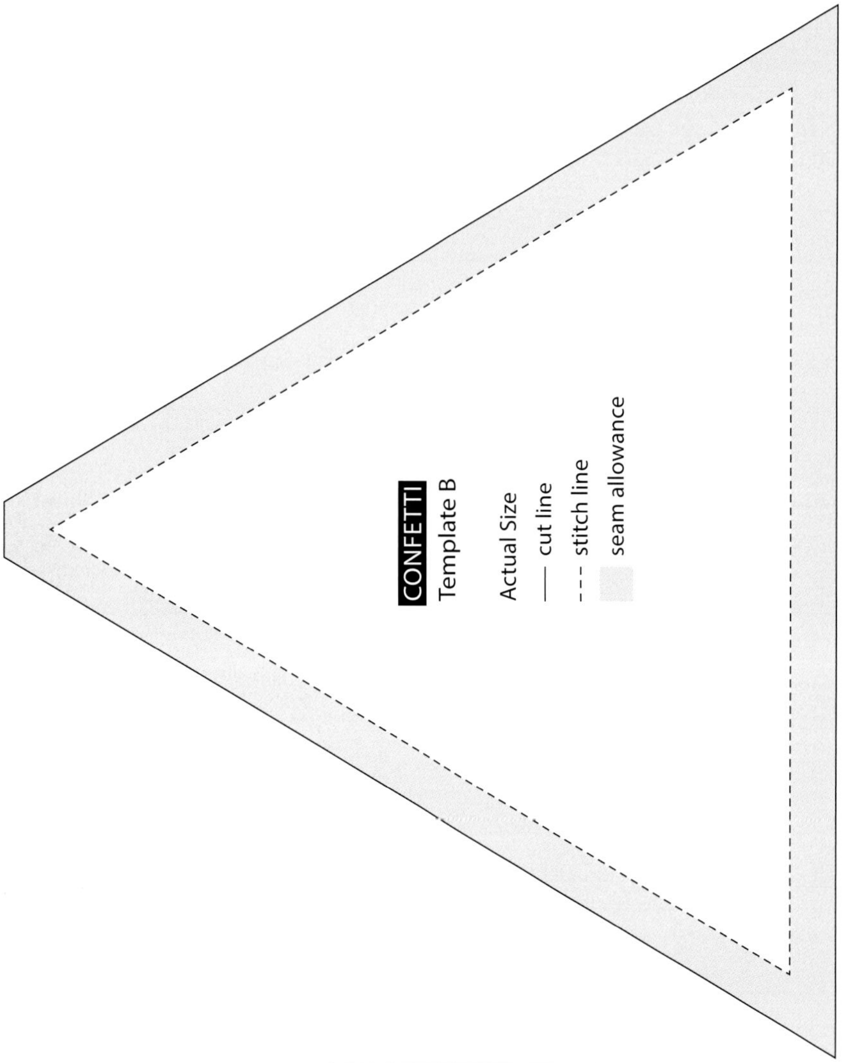
CONFETTI
Template B
Actual Size
cut line
stitch line
seam allowance

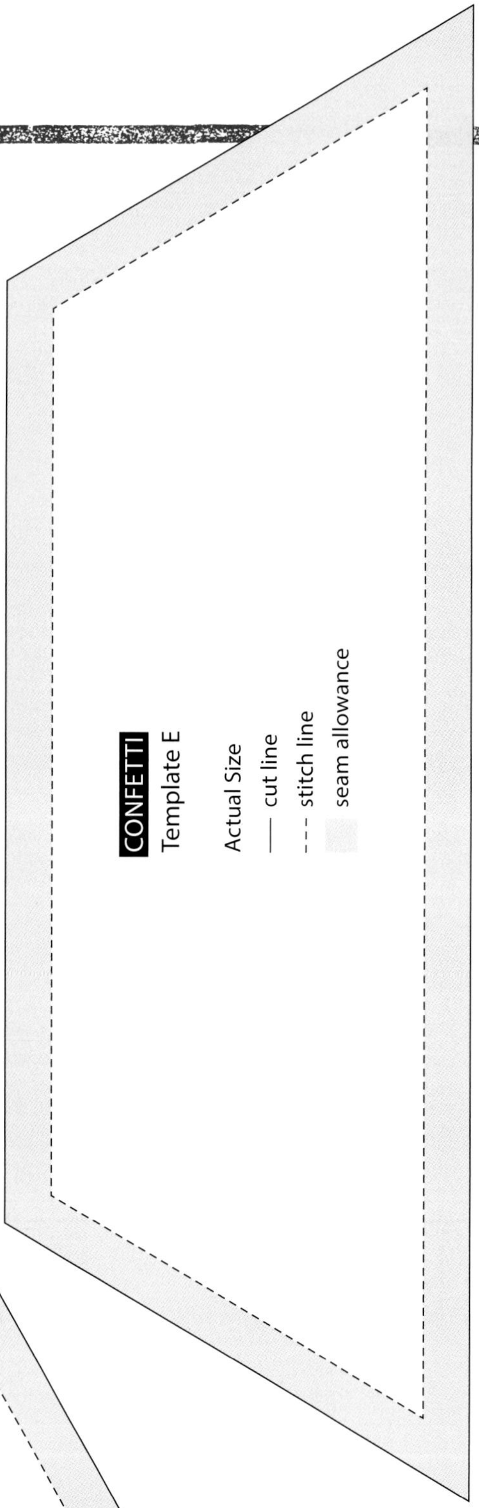
CONFETTI
Template E
Actual Size
cut line
stitch line
seam allowance

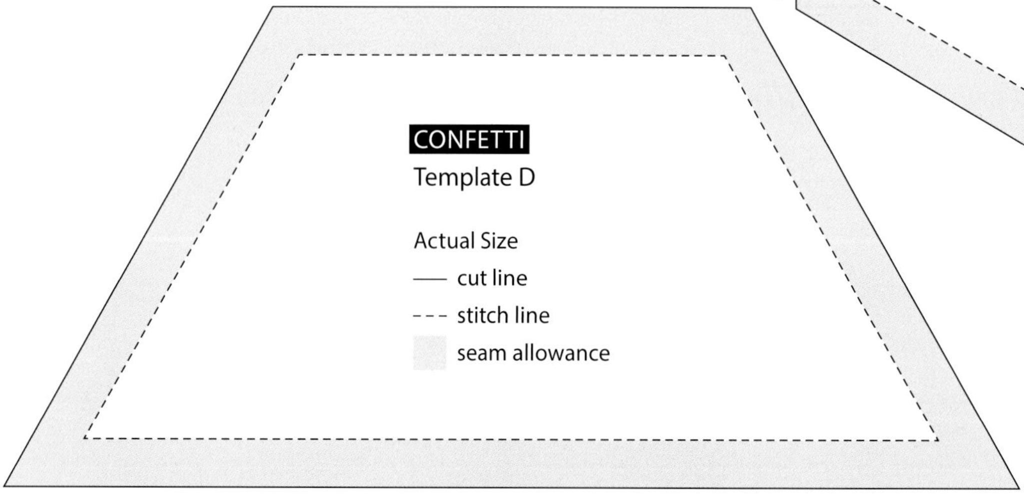
CONFETTI
Template D
Actual Size
cut line
stitch line
seam allowance

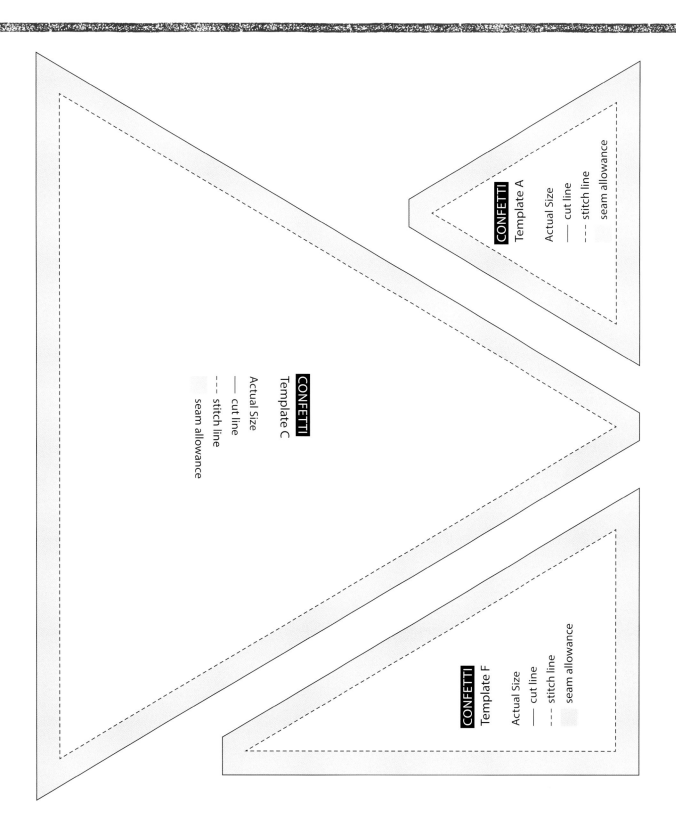

CONFETTI

Template A

Actual Size
—— cut line
- - - stitch line
▨ seam allowance

CONFETTI

Template C

Actual Size
—— cut line
- - - stitch line
▨ seam allowance

CONFETTI

Template F

Actual Size
—— cut line
- - - stitch line
▨ seam allowance

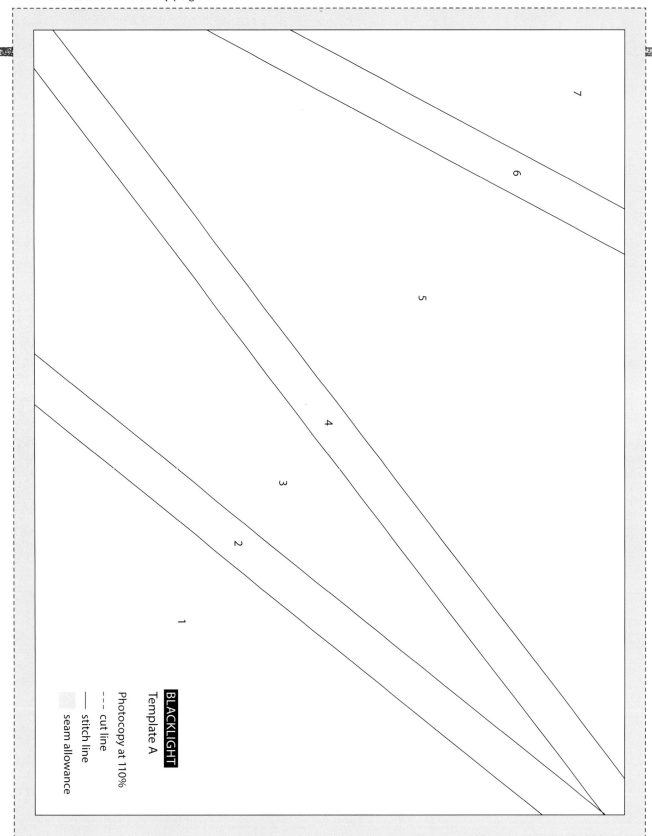

BLACKLIGHT
Template A

Photocopy at 110%

--- cut line
—— stitch line
seam allowance

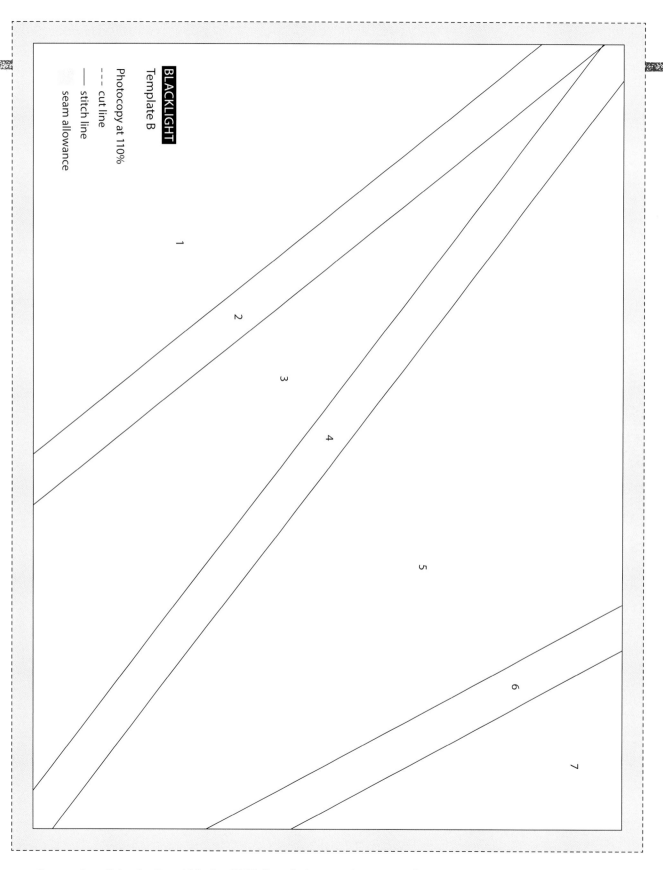

BLACKLIGHT

Template B

Photocopy at 110%

- - - cut line
— stitch line
seam allowance

1

2

3

4

5

6

7